DATE DUE			

UNIVERSITY
OF NORTH CAROLINA
STUDIES IN
COMPARATIVE
LITERATURE

NUMBER 47

UNIVERSITY OF NORTH CAROLINA
STUDIES IN COMPARATIVE LITERATURE

Founded by Werner P. Friederich

For Reprints from this Series see page 144.

GERMAN THOUGHT AND CULTURE IN ENGLAND

1700-1770

A PRELIMINARY SURVEY
INCLUDING A CHRONOLOGICAL BIBLIOGRAPHY
OF GERMAN LITERATURE IN ENGLISH TRANSLATION

BY

GAROLD N. DAVIS

CHAPEL HILL
THE UNIVERSITY OF NORTH CAROLINA PRESS
1969

001.20942
D29g
96810
april 1976

Printed in the Netherlands by Royal VanGorcum Ltd., Assen

ACKNOWLEDGMENTS

Anglo-German literary studies in America began in earnest with the work of Professor A. R. Hohlfeld at the University of Wisconsin in 1901. Since that time numerous dissertations, articles, and monographs on English, German, and American literary relations have been written under his direction or following his basic stimulus. Professor Hohlfeld has traced the early history of these studies in the „Forward" to his *Bibliography of German Literature in British Magazines* 1750-1860 and therein he states that by far most comprehensive and outstanding research in this field has been conducted by Professors B. Q. Morgan, Lawrence M. Price, and Harold Jantz. The present work, suggested and encouraged by Professor Harold Jantz, is thus a third generation offspring of the far-reaching project initiated by Professor Hohlfeld.

It is with pleasure that I acknowledge my gratitude to Professor Jantz, without whose advice (and excellent library) this book could not have been written. I am also grateful to Professors Ulrich Goldsmith and Albert Schmitt for reading the manuscript and offering helpful suggestions and criticisms. I also wish to express my appreciation to the Committee for University Scholarly Publications of the University of Colorado for so generously providing the necessary funds for publication. And no less important to me than the above has been the patient cooperation of my wife.

Provo, Utah, 1968   Garold N. Davis

TABLE OF CONTENTS

I. INTRODUCTION:
COMPARATIVE LITERATURE AND
THE THIRTY YEARS' WAR

In 1914 Gilbert Waterhouse called a kangaroo court into session for the purpose of trying Germany on charges of being a transmitter of foreign literature into England.[1] The defendant was acquitted. Since Germany was only a weak imitator of foreign models herself, he argued, and since she had been made incapable of literary activity by the Thirty Years' War, she would hardly be guilty of literary transmission or influence, and therefore the tedious task of further investigation was adjudged unnecessary. As the irony of life often orders such matters, two other scholars, Rufus M. Jones and Margaret L. Bailey, were making independent research in this same area. They published their conclusions the same year, and yet their verdict was the opposite of that of Gilbert Waterhouse.[2] Because of the chronology in this matter we can assume that Waterhouse was not aware of the concurrent Anglo-German studies of Jones and Bailey. He must have been aware of the recent work of Caroline Spurgeon on the influence of many German mystics in England,[3] and although she is not mentioned by Waterhouse, his book does contain a chapter in which he discusses the translations of Martin Luther and Jacob Boehme, but makes no effort to discuss the literary significance of these translations. This, of course, raises the question: With this important work in his own area of specialization going on around him, how is it possible that Waterhouse could reach the conclusion, to him quite logical, that a serious investigation of German cultural influences in England was unnecessary and that, in fact, the results that might be derived from any such investigation could be determined *a priori*? To answer this question is to explain much of the failure of Anglo-German studies of the past.

Joseph Walter, whom Waterhouse recommends as an authority on the German literature of the seventeenth century, approached the literature of this period by investigating the political and social conditions in Germany as they existed during the Thirty Years' War.[4] Now some modern critics might consider this a somewhat questionable method of literary scholarship, but Waterhouse is able to conclude from Joseph Walter's work: "That these years of war were unfavorable to the interests of literature is obvious." (xviii) Another writer recommended by Waterhouse is Georg Herzfeld who, in 1900 had written:

> It is well known that the works of Jacob Boehme were translated and disseminated in England in the seventeenth century, buf the interest in Boehme was, after all, theological, not literary.[5]

Waterhouse echoes this attitude in his short chapter on Luther and Boehme when he says: "The study of Luther's influence in England belongs more properly to the realm of theology than literature . . ." (95) These attitudes of Waterhouse and his precursors suggest an answer to our question. First, it was assumed as logical that because of the Thirty Years' War the quality of German literature would not merit international attention. And, second, the restrictive clause was attached to this assumption that anything drifting accidentally or incidentally into England from Germany that was of a religious nature did not count. Consequently, Waterhouse could conclude:

> The period [seventeenth century] has little attraction, as far as Germany is concerned, and receives scant attention in most histories of literature, — and with good reason, for the majority of the works of the age are absolutely worthless. (xii).

This attitude was unfortunately not restricted to the seventeenth century, and by applying the same type of logic one could conclude, as has been done, that "there was no literature in Germany worthy the name from . . . Luther . . . to Lessing."[6]

The idea that there was no significant literature in Germany worthy of notice in England until the late eighteenth century, and that this long period of cultural ineptitude in Germany was due in large measure to the Thirty Years' War was by no means original with Waterhouse, nor was Waterhouse the last scholar to have his vision obscured by this fable. The fable did persist, however. This unfortunate attitude toward German literature has not only misled scholars who might otherwise have discovered for themselves the wealth and beauty of German Baroque and Enlightenment literature, but it has also restrained scholars from making any serious investigation of the cultural relations between Germany and other countries during this time, except to show the "utter dependence" of Germany on foreign cultures. Only recently, through the efforts of scholars such as Jones, Spurgeon, and Bailey, who ironically were investigating cultural expressions other than the literary ones, and through the efforts of scholars such as Harold Jantz and Curt von Faber du Faur, whose investigations are more immediately concerned with German literature, have we been able to see German culture of the seventeenth and early eighteenth centuries without the obscuring *a priori* critical consensus of nearly 200 years. We are now beginning to see wherein and why so many scholars have failed to understand German Baroque and Enlightenment culture and we can consequently more clearly understand the international cultural relations of this period.

Since many of the scholars who arrived at the same conclusions as Waterhouse and Herzfeld were competent and highly esteemed in their field we cannot assume that their critical consensus was reached hastily or irresponsibly. But, this critical consensus was, in fact, invalid, and was primarily the result of a failure in scholarly and critical method: not one confined to this small area, but extending over large areas of comparative literary studies. Time and time again the same two basic critical fallacies have been in operation in regard to Anglo-German studies. 1. The scholars have tried to use an intellectual, logical approach to literary concerns, operating with "accepted" premises, categories, definitions, and limitations. For example, scholars have "logically" assumed that an adverse social condition within a country over a long period of time would have a deteriorating effect on the cultural expressions of that country. This has never been demonstrated to be a fact, and the cause and effect relationship involved is much too subtle for such a simple explanation. 2. Perhaps more serious than this "logical" approach has been the all too prevalent concept that literature is not related to other cultural manifestations. When, as was inevitable, there were scholars in other fields who did not know about this premise (Jones, Spurgeon, and Bailey for example) nor about the critical consensus that German influence in England was "illogical", and when they inadvertently or incidentally brought material to light that did demonstrate important literary influences at work, there were several ways of dealing with these intrusions. They could simply be overlooked, as they were in a number of instances that I will point out. If they could not be over-looked, they could be dismissed by definition and reduction. Devotional works in prose or verse belonged to religion, not literature. The fine arts and music, even the critical and aesthetic works in these fields, had no literary relevance. And, of course, scientific, political, diplomatic, and personal relations would be quite without literary significance. The *a priori* limitation to "purely" literary concerns involves a basic assumption that literature grows in air-tight and isolated compartments, isolated, that is, from the larger cultural environment. However, this assumption overlooks the fact that lyric poetry is often a musical expression and that hymn writing is a religious expression. These attempts to isolate literature from other

3

cultural manifestations of life only place blinders on the scholar and are bound to lead to misunderstanding and faulty conclusions.

If we replace these *a priori* assumptions and exclusions with a method of *a posteriori* conclusions from phenomena observed in context, if we first look at what is there, note the relations, and only then decide whether they have literary relavence or not, we obtain remarkably different results. But, in the case of Anglo-German relations this has not been done. A brief history of the major Anglo-German scholarship will illustrate this point.

Otto Weddigen in 1878 stated that "awareness of German language and literature in England before the end of the previous century was either very slight or non-existent."[7] Weddigen cites Macaulay as the source of this information, assuming, it appears, the Macaulay had made a thorough investigation of the situation. In 1897 Leslie Stephen perpetuates this idea: "Macaulay remarks that the members of Johnson's Club were ignorant of the very existence of Wieland or Lessing."[8] Thus we learn from Weddigen that the language and literature of Germany were not known in England, and we learn from Stephen that the members of "Johnson's Club" had never even heard of Wieland or Lessing, and both Weddingen and Stephen cite Macaulay as the source of their information. Let us see just what Macaulay did say.

In the "Life and Writings of Addison" published in 1843 Macaulay discusses Addison's surprise on hearing from Boileau, then an old man, that he (Boileau) knew nothing of the contemporary English literature. Looking for an analogy Macaulay writes:

> English literature was to the French of the age of Lewis the Fourteenth what German literature was to our own grandfathers. Very few, we suspect, of the accomplished man who, sixty or seventy years ago, used to dine in Leicester Square with Sir Joshua, or at Streatham with Mrs. Thrale, had the slightest notion that Wieland was one of the first wits and poets, and Lessing, beyond all dispute, the first critic in Europe.[9]

What Macaulay says here is not that "the members of Johnson's Club were ignorant of the very existence of Wieland or Lessing," nor that awareness in England of the language and literature of Germany was non-existent. What he says is that very few of the men who dined with Sir Joshua or with Mrs. Thrale had as yet recognized the true stature of Wieland and Lessing in European letters. Actually, Macaulay does not even say this authoritatively, but in making his analogy with the Frenchmen's ignorance writes: "we suspect ..." That is, Macaulay admits that he had made no detailed investigation of the German-English relations of this period but is only putting forth his opinion for what it is worth. This opinion was evidently worth a great deal to Leslie Stephen, however, who concludes:

> It is a familiar fact that no Englishman read German literature in the eighteenth
> century. One sufficient reason was that there was no German literature to read . . .
> It would, I imagine, be difficult to find a single direct reference to a German book
> in the whole English literature of the eighteenth century. (42)

Addison was surprised that Boileau was ignorant of contemporary English literature so Macaulay suspects that few accomplished men of his grandfather's generation were aware of Wieland or Lessing, and thus Otto Weddigen and Leslie Stephen can report that no one in England in the eighteenth century read German literature! What kind of history is that? It is, of course, no history at all, but the thesis had by this time been repeated so often that it was accepted as history, and with a little embellishment, comparative literature is turned into a merchandising metaphor. In 1901 Ernst Margraf writing of the German literature of the late eighteenth and early nineteenth centuries says:

> In former periods and even at the beginning of her greatness German literature
> lived a miserable life of imitation and servitude. Now, however, she could repay
> England all the capital she had borrowed, and with compounded interest.[10]

In 1907 Thomas George Tucker also approaches comparative literature as an economist with his book: *The Foreign Debt of English Literature*. In introducing German literature and discussing England's "debt" Tucker echoes Margraf when he says: "But to Germany we owed an inconsiderable debt until the end of the eighteenth century or the beginning of the nineteenth . . ."[11] Literary "debt" has now become a quantitative thing, and as such it is an easy matter, and a logical one to Tucker, to dispose of the German Baroque, Enlightenment, Rococo, and Storm and Stress literature. We start in the sixteenth century and "with a long leap over an irrelevant and wearisome interspace we arrive at the Classic period of German literature."[12] Three years later we hear the same story, that "in the seventeenth century England could receive no literary stimulation from Germany, as Germany had been laid waste by the Thirty-Years War."[13]

And so, by the time of Gilbert Waterhouse we are no longer dealing with the history of an idea, but with the history of a cliché, and Waterhouse feels that he owes his readers an explanation as to why he is investigating seventeenth century German literature at all.

> The period has little attraction, as far as Germany is concerned . . . for the majority
> of the works of the age are absolutely worthless . . . The object, therefore, of
> the present volume is not to claim that German literature of the seventeenth
> century is, after all, worth reading for its own sake, but simply to trace the literary
> relations of England and Germany from the sixteenth century to the eighteenth.
> (xii)

The next major treatment of German-English literary relations was F. W. Stokoe's *German Influence in the English Romantic Period* (Cambridge, 1926). Although Stokoe's book is supposed to deal with the late eighteenth and early nineteenth centuries, he does not fail to offer his opinion on the early eighteenth century, and once again we have a host of stock phrases and generalizations about a period that he has not investigated. Germany in the early eighteenth century was "incapable of spontaneous effort, of any considerable originality." and the country could be described as being in the "likeness of a stammering boor." "A long trance . . . had befallen its intellectual life." (2) The only literary men in Germany were Lessing and Klopstock. Again in 1927 we hear the familiar sounds, when Laurie Magnus continued the tradition of avoiding a study of the seventeenth and early eighteenth centuries by merely referring to the Thirty Years' War, as if that explained everything. Germany was in a "slough of despond."[14]

In 1929 Violet A. Stockley published *German Literature as known in England* 1750-1830 (London, 1929). Although the title of her work indicates an interest in German literature from 1750, her main thesis is that "though isolated German works had English readers before 1790, yet not until after that date was there in England anything like a real appreciation of the general development of German literature." (1,2) Rather than expand this idea and explain just what is meant by a "general development of German literature," Mrs. Stockley simply refers to the previous "studies" of the early eighteenth century and then presents four reasons why there could not have been any literary stimulation coming from Germany.

> First: All through the seventeenth and first half of the eighteenth centuries, when France was at the height of her literary fame, Germany had no literature worth international notice. Politically, she had been weak and divided since the Thirty Years' War; her arms had fallen into disrepute, and also indirectly her language. (2)

Here is another attempt to make a judgment on a body of literature by drawing conclusions from the field of politics.

> Second: As far as foreign literatures were concerned French literature and style were dominant in England, and French opinion was accepted without question in most branches of literature. (2)

> Third: Ignorance of the German language, commonly regarded as presenting almost insurmountable difficulties to a foreigner. (2)

Mrs. Stockley does not present any evidence to support these statements but simply quotes an absurd analogy from the *Edinburgh Review*, XXIII (1813), 198: "Thirty years ago [i.e. 1783] there were probably in London as many Persian as German scholars." The "probably" here indicates another opinion that has been accepted as fact, and it might have been a surprise to Mrs. Stockley to learn that throughout the 18th century there were German scholars in London and that German literature was being translated and published during that time in increasing frequency.

> Fourth: The scarcity of German books. The great expense of printing in England hindered reprints and the exorbitant duty on foreign books hindered importation. (3).

This duty on books must have been a hardship only on those trying to get German literature since "French literature and style were dominant in England."

Mrs. Stockley then presents four reasons for the gradual rise in interest in German literature and its introduction into England around 1790.

> First: The number of German officers in the English army during the American War (1775-83), who spread some knowledge of their language and literature among their English comrades. Second: a certain amount of court encouragement for German works. George III married a German princess, Charlotte of Mecklenburg, in 1760, and several early translations . . . are dedicated "to the Queen." Third: The growing interest in France for German literature . . . Fourth: The activity of Germans resident in England. (4,5)

It is ironic that Mrs. Stockley should choose these four reasons for the increased interest in German literature in the *latter* part of the century, and at the same time speak about the lack of interest in German literature in the *earlier* part of the century. She mentions the German soldiers in England during the "American War," but is apparently unaware of the thousands of German Palatines in London in 1709 and the numerous Salzburgers in London in the 1730s. She mentions court encouragement for German literature by reminding us that George III married a German princess but she fails to mention that the court had been German since 1714, and with much closer ties to Germany than the court of George III. Nor does she mention court encouragement from Queen Anne and her husband, Prince George, who surrounded himself with German Pietists. She mentions the "Germans resident in England" who were active in spreading German culture and literature, but she fails to mention the many translators active before 1760. She says nothing about the many Germans active in the Royal Society from its beginning nor about the many German musicians, artists, and theologians who were living in England during this period. She mentions none of these things, of course, because her study does not concern itself with this earlier period. Like so many scholars before her, however, she feels qualified to describe the literary conditions in a period she has not studied and to state conclusions from research that has never been made. Again, it must be stressed that the many scholars who have reached such negative conclusions with such a minimum of investigation into the problems were not incompetent scholars, nor did they arrive at their conclusions without thought. The fact is, that thought often became a substitute for research. Gilbert Waterhouse has outlined some very important material concerning the English influences in Germany in the seventeenth century, and his extensive bibliography is very valuable for further research. Likewise, Violet Stockley has done an adequate job of furnishing us with a general survey of the Anglo-German relations during the first decades of the nineteenth century. Only when their studies of German literature are based on "logic" instead of scholarship does their work fail to achieve the objective.

The fallacious ideas concerning the Thirty Years' War and the strange concept of "pure" literature were two critical postulates which had been accepted and repeated so long and so often that it was evidently impossible to see objectively what had and what had not been done. Even the very great scholars Alexander Hohlfeld and B. Q. Morgan, after the extensive and very significant work they had done in Anglo-German relations, were unable to see clearly through the obstructing concepts that stood before them. In the introduction to their combined work *"German Literature in British Magazines* 1750-1860 (Madison, 1949) they have reiterated almost point by point the conclusions presented by Violet Stockley twenty years earlier.

Having presented a somewhat negative overview of the nature of the scholarship concerned with Anglo-German relations I must mention some of the more positive work that has been done. B. Q. Morgan's *Bibliography of German Literature in English Translation,* now available with a *Supplement* bringing the translations up to 1955, is the most complete bibliography of translations of German literature. The present organization of the bibliography makes it somewhat difficult to use for research into specific periods of literary history, and it is not complete, especially in the periods before 1800, but, used with caution, it is the most helpful and objective tool yet available for Anglo-German studies. Also, the Morgan-Hohlfeld *German Literature in British Magazines,* with the exception of the misleading introduction mentioned above, has valuable information, but only for the second half of the eighteenth century and the first half of the nineteenth. The most extensive history of the German culture in England has been written by Karl Heinrich Schaible, but the quality of his work is quite uneven. As an introduction to the chapter on the eighteenth century Schaible excuses his failing:

> I must sadly admit, that in this chapter I fail to mention not only important German individuals but whole groups of such . . .
>
> As a consequence of my absence from England it was not possible for me to follow the same plan in this chapter that I carried out in the first five chapters; that is, not only to give a biographical sketch of individual Germans but also to give a picture of the German-English relations and to sketch out the influence of our countrymen in England.[15]

8

Schaible mentions the complex relationship between England and Germany that existed in the eighteenth century as a result of the Hannoverian occupation of the English throne, and he expresses his intention of completing his history by making a more thorough investigation of the eighteenth century, but unfortunately this was never done.

I have mentioned the names of Rufus Jones, Margaret L. Bailey, and Caroline Spurgeon for their work with Jacob Boehme and the German mystics. Since their time other works of a like nature have been published but no attempt has yet been made to unify the studies of this influence into a coherency, which, in view of the subject matter, is no easy task. Marjorie Nicholson has mentioned some German relations with England in the seventeenth and eighteenth centuries in her books *The Breaking of the Circle*, *Voyages to the Moon*, and *Mountain Gloom and Mountain Glory*, but her major concern is not literary relations as such. Suggestions, however, from such a significant scholar as Marjorie Nicholson should make us aware that there is much more to be done in this area. G. H. Turnbull has recently thrown much light on the German-English relations in the seventeenth century by his survey of the papers of Samuel Hartlib.[16] Professor Harold Jantz has been kind enough to show me an unpublished paper entitled "Unexplored Phases of German Influence on Seventeenth-Century English Literature," and this paper mentions German influences on such important writers as John Donne, John Milton, Robert Burton, John Bunyan, Francis Bacon, and Isaac Newton, to mention but a few. James Taft Hatfield has written on John Wesley's translation of German hymns, as has Henry Bett.[17] a subject I will treat more fully in Chapter II.

With few exceptions, however, literary s c h o l a r s tracing German literature in England have avoided the seventeenth and early eighteenth centuries. To make this study more difficult, such important reference works as Wing's *Short Title Catalogue*, the *McAlpin Collection* in the Union Theological Seminary, and the *Term Catalogues* all terminate at about 1700.

How, then, is one to approach this entire area of literary history where so much has been written but so little investigated? The only logical approach is that approach outlined by Harold Jantz in his very important article on German Baroque literature.[18] We must first sweep aside all the obscuring clichés and pseudomorphs concerning the Thirty Years' War and all the *a priori* conclusions concerning German culture drawn from these clichés and pseudomorphs. We must ignore the narrow, limiting, and prejudicial writings which make attempts to isolate literature from other cultural expressions, with their consequent negative results. We must make as broad and comprehensive a survey of this period as possible, taking note of

9

personal relations and contacts, German theologians, scientists, musicians, artists, and travellers. We must investigate all the translations from German to English from all fields. We must be comprehensive and not exclusive. This is the first step. Then, with the Anglo-German cultural relations of the eighteenth century placed in their proper historical perspective, we shall be able to draw logical *a posteriori* conclusions. We shall be able to compare and contrast, examine and evaluate, and present a true historical picture. Then will follow comprehensive surveys of the emerging patterns and their literary relevance, and along with these surveys will come probes in depth into the more significant and serious aspects of these cultural relations. The present work is admittedly a beginning. It is an attempt to place into their historical order the primary facts concerning German culture in England within the period 1700-1770. As a first survey there are many inferences but few conclusions, some evidence but no final verdict.

II. THE SPIRITUAL LYRIC
BECOMES SECULAR:
THE TRANSLATION AND RECEPTION
OF THE GERMAN HYMN

An oft repeated but unfounded theory for the supposed lack of foreign interest in German literature during the period under discussion is the theory that there was no German literature. Or, to recall the words of Mrs. Stockley: "All through the seventeenth and the first half of the eighteenth centuries, when France was at the height of her literary fame, Germany had no literature worth international notice." Does Mrs. Stockley actually mean what she says, or does she really mean: "All through the seventeenth and first half of the eighteenth centuries, . . . Germany had no literature that *received* international notice." Perhaps the distinction is irrelevant, since both statements are false.

Forgetting for the moment all other literary genres, German lyric poetry was worthy of and did receive a great deal of notice, especially in England and particularly in the early eighteenth century. To reply that lyric poetry in seventeenth and eighteenth-century England was not considered to be on the same level of literary importance with the drama or even with the novel is to miss the point. Toward the end of the eighteenth century lyric poetry in English literature experienced a revitilization that has made this genre one of the most significant mediums of literary expression to our day, and the resurgent interest in the lyric poem in England in the late eighteenth century was to a relatively large extent a result of the continuing interest in the lyric poem in Germany and the high quality of German lyric poetry from the middle ages, through the eighteenth century, to the present. And to say that spiritual lyric poetry, the hymn, is not to be considered in the same literary class with secular lyric poetry is also to miss the point. There is no logical reason to assume that Charles Wesley's great hymn "Jesus Lover of my Soul" is any more "literary" when published in an anthology of eighteenth century English verse for exegesis by undergraduates than when published in a Methodist hymn book for an emotional stimulation and for subtle doctrinal propaganda. Nor is there any logical reason to assume that a poet's expression of passionate love for the "Bridegroom of the soul" is any less literary than "My Love is like a Red Red Rose," or "Du bist wie eine Blume." There are distinctions, but not distinctions in genre. Even omitting all other literary genres, one can certainly say that Germany did have a literature "worth international notice" in the seventeenth and eighteenth centuries.

In this chapter I have outlined the historical movement of the spiritual lyric into England—continually pointing out the importance of this phenomenon for the rejuvenation of English lyric poetry of the late eighteenth and early nineteenth centuries. One should not assume, however, that the quality of German literature in the seventeenth and eighteenth centuries is to be evaluated solely on the basis of the output of lyric poetry. I do believe, however, it is evident that the lyric poem in the history of German literature has been the most constant genre, and for our present concern it is also the most significant.

Germany has always stood pre-eminent in both the quantity and quality of lyric poetry, and it is just at the time period mentioned by Mrs. Stockley that the spiritual lyric in Germany reached new heights that have not often been equaled and never surpassed. John Julian, the learned and careful scholar of English hymnody has said:

> German hymnody surpasses all others in wealth. The Church hymn . . . was born with the German Reformation, and most extensively cultivated ever since by the evangelical church in Germany.

> The number of German hymns cannot fall short of one hundred thousand . . . Many of these hymns, and just those possessed of the greatest vigour and the richest comfort, had their origin amid the conflicts and storms of the Reformation, or the fearful devastations and nameless miseries of the Thirty Years' War; others belong to the revival period of the Spenerian Pietism and the Moravian Brotherhood, and reflect its earnest struggle after holiness, the fire of the first love and the sweet enjoyment of the soul's intercourse with her Heavenly Bridegroom; not a few of them sprang up even in the unbelieving age of "illumination" and rationalism, like flowers from dry ground, or Alpine roses on fields of snow; others again proclaim, in fresh and joyous tones, the dawn of reviving faith in the land where the Reformation had its birth.[1]

As a more specific refutation of Mrs. Stockley's charges I need only mention the following—all esteemed as poets from a purely literary-critical point of view: Philip Nicolai (1522-1608), Johannes Heermann (1585-1647), Martin Rinckart (1586-1649), Friedrich von Spee (1591-1635), Johann Rist (1607-1667), Paul Gerhardt (1607-1676), Angelus Silesius (1624-1677), Joachim Neander (1650-1680), Ernst Lange (1650-1727), Johann Freylinghausen (1670-1739), Johann Andreas

Rothe (1688-1758), Gerhard Tersteegen (1697-1769), and Nicholas Ludwig von Zinzendorf (1700-1760). Verse from all of these writers and many others was translated into English in the eighteenth century.

The English hymn had its beginnings according to some literary historians with Bishop Ken in the late seventeenth century, while others ascribe the first real hymns to Isaac Watts. There are some who say that the English hymn was really born as late as the 1740s with the hymns of Charles Wesley. This problem, like other problems of origin, revolves on the meaning of the word "beginning." One could probably with some justification say that the English hymn began with Caedmon and has continued in an unbroken chain to the present. Many of the Latin hymns of the middle-ages have found their way into the present-day hymn books, having gone through various translations along the route. An example is the beloved "English" hymn, "Jesus, the very thought of Thee with sweetness fills my breast." This hymn is a translation of *Jesu dulcis memoria*, written about 1130, perhaps by Bernard of Clairvaux. It was translated into English in at least seven different version between 1712 and 1760, all stemming from three German translations of the Latin original. The three German translations of the original with their English translations are:

1. "Ach Gott, wie manches Herzeleid," by Martin Moller, 1578, translated and published as:

   a. "O Lord! how many miseries," by J. C. Jacobi, 1720, 1722, 1732.

   b. "O God, how many an anxious hour," in the Moravian hymn book of 1754.

2. "O Jesu süss, wer dein gedenkt," from the 1612 edition of Johann Arndt's *Paradies-Gärtlein* (though perhaps not by Arndt), translated and published as:

   a. "When memory brings Jesus to my sense," by Anton Wilhelm Boehm, appended to the English Translation of Arndt's *True Christianity*, 1712.

   b. "When thought brings Jesus to my sense," a revision of the above by Johann Christian Jacobi, 1720, 1722.

   c. "Sweet Jesus when I think on thee," an alteration of the above by Jacobi, 1732, and in the Moravian hymn book of 1754.

   d. "Of him who did salvation bring," the third stanza of Jacobi's 1732 version in Madan's *Psalms and Hymns*, 1760.

3. "Jesu, deiner zu gedenken," by Nicholas Ludwig Zinzendorf, 1731, translated and published as:

   a. "Jesu, on Thee to be thinking," in the Moravian hymn book of 1754.

The history of "Jesu dulcis memoria" is interesting in itself but it also illustrates the difficulty that arises when we attempt to find a beginning for the hymn and when we attempt to limit the term "hymn" to mean only the spiritual poetry that was "to be sung by the congregation in

13

public worship." (Julian, 412) Many hymns, such as the one under discussion, were not written for public worship at all, and although they are now used for that purpose, they are still read and appreciated as literature by people who have only a nodding acquaintance with public worship.

Every poem loses some of its quality in the process of translation, but with the translation of spiritual poetry, there is very often also a quality gained, depending, of course, on the genius of the translator. The original Latin form of "Jesu dulcis memoria" is still identifiable in Jacobi's "Sweet Jesus when I think on Thee," even though we are reading (or singing) an alteration of a revision of an English translation of a German translation of the Latin original! Spiritual poetry has the power to survive translation, and this power often seems to be lacking or at least rare in other forms of verse. The German translations of Shakespeare show their age after a few decades and must be revised, and in spite of the many translations of Goethe's *Faust*, no one seems to have captured the quality of the original. In the case of spiritual poetry, however, there is many an example of a translation that has exhibited the power to transcend both time and language barriers and to be accepted in its new environment as a natural, original, indigenous work. Thus Clifford Towlson can rightly say of Johann Andreas Rothe's hymn, "Ich habe nun den Grund gefunden": "It is a magnificent hymn of faith in adversity which Wesley has made even more magnificent in "Now I have found the Ground."[2]

This easy and rapid assimilation of spiritual poetry in translation creates a problem, however, for anyone attempting to discuss "influences." The inflowing stream of spiritual poetry from Germany in the eighteenth century had a discernible effect on English spiritual poetry and on the general cultural pattern. After this initial influence, however, it is difficult to find again the elements that brought about this change; that is, it is difficult to distinguish German hymnody in its new environment from native English hymnody. Charles Wesley's hymns reveal the same spirit that had inspired John Wesley's translations from the German. Perhaps the safest ground, then, in discussing origins is to say that English spiritual poetry had its origins with the first recorded literature in the language and has continued to the present. There have been times in the history of English letters, however, when this spiritual poetry has rapidly increased in quantity and has shown new and interesting qualities. The greatest stimulation to this spiritual verse came about through the introduction of congregational singing in the churches. Hymns had been sung in the churches before the reformation, but not usually by the congregation. This practice, established and encouraged by Martin Luther, spread rapidly from Germany to other countries, and one of the

14

first signs of this influence in England was the appearance of Miles Coverdale's *Goostly Psalmes and Spiritual Songs* (1539), all but five of which have been traced to their German origin. (Julian, 442) Unfortunately the practice of hymn singing was restricted in England before it became really well established, and with very few exceptions the protestant churches in England turned to the Psalms for their musical inspiration. Toward the end of the seventeenth century a few of the dissenting congregations began singing hymns again, and in 1691 Benjamin Keach published *The Breach Repaired in God's Worship; or Singing of Psalms, Hymns and Spiritual Songs proved to be a Holy Ordinance of Jesus Christ.* Contrary to Keach's wishes, however, the breach was not repaired and hymn singing was frowned upon by many churches until well into the eighteenth century and beyond.

With the hymns of Isaac Watts, which he began publishing in 1706, the singing of spiritual songs other than the Psalms became more common, and the publication of spiritual poetry began to increase. It was just at this crucial moment in the history of English hymnody that the German spiritual lyric began to make its influence felt once again in England.

In 1708 there was published in London a volume of hymns with the title: *Lyra Davidica, or a Collection of Divine Songs and Hymns, partly new composed, partly translated from the High German and Latin Hymns; and set to Easy and Pleasant Tunes*, (London, J. Walsh). No one seems to know anything about the authorship of this collection of hymns, and it has become so rare that in all my searching I have not yet located a copy. Julian says that "the character of its contents may perhaps lead to the supposition that it was compiled by some Anglo-German of the Pietist school of thought." The leader of the pietist school of thought in London in 1708 was Anton Wilhelm Boehm, the chaplain for Prince George. Boehm's life is discussed in Chapter III. He had been active in translating from German into English since 1705 when he translated and published August Wilhelm Francke's *Pietas Hallensis*, and in 1712 Boehm showed his abilities as a translator of verse when he included a translation of Arndt's "O Jesu süss wer dein gedenkt" in his publication of *True Christianity*. There is no direct evidence that Boehm had anything to do with the translation or publication of the *Lyra Davidica*, but it is very unlikely that he was either unaware of or unconcerned with its publication and distribution.

Another likely candidate for the honors is Johann Christian Jacobi, who had been in London for some time and who in 1708, the year of the publication of the translation, had been made keeper of the Royal German Chapel at St. James where Boehm was Court Chaplain. The close affiliation between Jacobi and Boehm could suggest a collaboration, but there is no external evidence that such was the case. Jacobi was one of the first and most gifted translators of German verse in the eighteenth century, but the first of his acknowledged translations was not published until 1720.

The preface to the *Lyra Davidica* expresses the desire that "a freer air than psalm-tunes might be acceptable." These sentiments suggest another hymn writer who was working for the same objectives in 1708, namely, Isaac Watts. There is also no external evidence that he was associated with the project, but he was a good friend of Johann Christian Jacobi, and he would certainly have had every reason to lend his support and influence to any project that attempted to make acceptable a "freer air than psalm-tunes."

Isaac Watts was not unknown in the Pietistic circles at Halle from where both Jacobi and Boehm had come. Johann Jacob Rambach, Boehm's biographer and editor, refers to him as the "unter uns nicht unbekante Herr Isaac Watts." Rambach had written the preface to one of Isaac Watts' religious tracts that had been translated and published at Halle in 1727 as "Tod und Himmel."[3] This event, of course, has nothing to do with the translation and publication of the *Lyra Davidica* in 1708, except perhaps to indicate that Isaac Watts' connections with the German Pietists have been generally overlooked. In editing the writings of Boehm, Rambach included a letter written by Isaac Watts to Johann Christian Jacobi on the occasion of Boehm's death in 1721. Because of the interesting light in throws on the relations between Watts, Jacobi, and Boehm, I quote it here in part.

> I most heartily condole with you the loss of so excellent a Man as Mr. Boehm; the Tidings shook me with a painful Surpise: [sic] I fear there are but few such Men in the Ministry, British or German, Episcopal or Nonconformist, & c . . . None could value and honour such a Man more heartily than my self. I am sorry my small Portion of Health is so necessarily filled up, and imployed in twenty other Things, that I cannot possibly undertake the Translation of his *Enchiridion Precum*: I wish it done by a better Hand. His Opinion of Prayer in the Introduction is so entirely the same with what I have long embraced, that I take Pleasure in finding a Person of such uncommon Piety in one Sentiment with my self:[4]

In 1735 Jacobi published a translation of Rambach's life of Boehm.[5] The translation contains a "Recommendation" written by Isaac Watts in which Watts indicates that Boehm had been the inspiration for one of the characters in his *Miscellaneous Thoughts*.

> And since his Friends have found it out, I will now confess that he [Boehm] was the Person from whom I borrowed that Character in my late Miscellaneous Thoughts, No. 52. where I represent a Reconciler between the rigid Extremes of Opinion, which are held by some of the Church of England and some of the Protestant Dissenters, relating to Forms of Prayer.

Returning to the *Lyra Davidica*, there were many other possible translators in London at this time, including John King, "master of both languages," who had published a *Compleat English Guide for*

High Germans in 1706, which was, among other things, a German-English dictionary. Nicholas Staphorst had been busy in 1706 translating a collection of travels from the "High Dutch" that were published by John Ray, and in 1700 Charles Hoole had translated *Sensualium Pictus* by J. A. Comenius from "Latin and High Dutch."

The author of the *Lyra Davidica*, whoever he was, showed discrimination in the selection of hymns, for it is in this volume that Philip Nicolai's two great hymns first appeared in English translation. "Wie schön leuchtet der Morgenstern" was translated as "How fairly shines the Morning Star," and "Wachet auf, ruft uns die Stimme" was translated as "Awake, the voice is crying." The latter was the favorite hymn of Philip Jacob Spener, "the father of Pietism," and was consequently very popular among the Pietists. In addition to these two beautiful hymns the *Lyra Davidica* also contained the popular anthem "Christ the Lord is Risen Today, Halleluia," a translation of the Latin "Surrexit Christus hodie." Martin Luther's "Komm heiliger Geist, Herre Gott," was translated as "Come holy, holy Ghost, Lord our God." Two other popular hymns that first appeared in English through the *Lyra Davidica* are: "Freu dich sehr, o meine Seele," as "Rouse thyself, my Soul, endeavour," and J. C. Lange's "Mein Herzens-Jesu, meine Lust," as "Sweet Jesus who my wish fulfills."

The author of the article on the hymn in *Grove's Dictionary of Music and Musicians* speaks disapprovingly of the type of influence exerted by the *Lyra Davidica*, and his remark is enlightening. In discussing the stated attempt of the author to make acceptable a "freer air than psalm tunes" he states:

> The freest air given is the familiar "Jesus Christ is risen today, Allelujah." The hymn is such a favorite that one can but judge it indulgently. In its purest form, as given in *Songs of Sion* (1905), it is a good deal less florid than in the usual version, nevertheless it marks the introduction of a new and frivolous spirit into English hymn-tunes, which gradually spread throughout the 18th century and had disastrous results.[6]

This author express his opinion that these hymns and their tunes introduced a "new and frivolous spirit" and that this spirit spread throughout the century. As suggested in the introduction to this chapter, it is difficult to trace the influence of spiritual poetry, except by observing the immediate results it may have had on the general direction of the literary currents. The *Lyra Davidica* appeared just at the time Isaac Watts was also attempting to make "a freer air than psalm-tunes" more acceptable, and these two voices soon became one in the general chorus.

The fact that the *Lyra Davidica* was known to hymnologists up to the middle of the eighteenth century is made evident by John Arnold's *Compleat Psalmodist* (second edition, 1749) which contains the first stanza of "Jesus Christ is risen today" from the translation in the

Lyra Davidica. The music to which the hymn was set in the *Compleat Psalmodist* is the music that was published with the hymn in the *Lyra Davidica* and is the music to which the song is still sung today. Also, Charles Wesley's "Christ the Lord is Risen Today," was likely inspired by this hymn, at least Samuel Duffield, a nineteenth century scholar of English hymnody, says that the 1708 version "may easily have been the suggestion from which Wesley's lyric came."[7] When Charles Wesley wrote "Christ the Lord is Risen Today" in 1739 he was strongly under the influence of German hymns and music. It is not unlikely that he knew the *Lyra Davidica*, and it is certain that he knew the German translations of J. C. Jacobi that were first published in 1720.

After the *Lyra Davidica* the next major translations of German hymns were those by Johann Christian Jacobi, who by this time had become Court Musician at St. James. As mentioned, Jacobi was a good friend of Isaac Watts, but how active Watts was in advancing the cause of German hymnody is unknown. Watts did participate with Jacobi on the *Psalmodia Germanica* (1722) by allowing Jacobi to use some of his hymns.

> I have, with the Leave of the Reverend Mr. Watts, transcrib'd one entire Hymn out of his *Horae Lyricae*, upon the Nativity of Christ, and the 127 Psalm, out of his new Translation; both of which agree so well with our German Composures on those subjects, that I made bold to try, how a good English Verse, set to a German tune, might be relish'd by a British Singer.[8]

Watts' hymn on the nativity mentioned by Jacobi is "Shepherds rejoyce, lift up your eyes, "and is set to the music of Nicholas Hermann's "Lobt Gott ihr Christen, alle gleich." The 127th Psalm by Watts is the one beginning, "Is God withdrawing, all the cost and pains that build the house are lost." The collection actually contains still another hymn by Watts not specifically mentioned by Jacobi: "He reigns, the Lord our Saviour Reigns." This hymn is set to the music of Luther's "Vom Himmel hoch da komm ich her."

In all, there were five publications of Jacobi's translations in the eighteenth century. The first called *A Collection of Divine Hymns* was published in 1720 and contained fifteen hymns. (For complete titles see Supplement). In 1722 this was expanded to sixty-two hymns under the title *Psalmodia Germanica; or a Specimen of Divine Hymns*. Part Two of the *Psalmodia Germanica* was issued in 1725. In 1732, the 1722 and 1725 editions were combined as *Psalmodia Germanica . . . 2nd edition, corrected and enlarged*. In 1765 John Haberkorn published a *Psalmodia Germanica . . . 3rd edition* with a "Supplement to German Psalmody". This was a republication of the 1732 edition with a supplement of thirty-two hymns by Haberkorn. All of these editions were printed "together with their proper tunes and thorough bass."

Both the dedication and the preface to the 1722 edition reveal interesting facts concerning the translation of these German hymns. The dedication is addressed to "their Royal Highnesses, Princess Anne, Princess Amalia, and Princess Carolina," and it states in part:

> The following sheets exhibit a translation of psalmody, used in the native country of Your Royal Highnesses, which (as well as other protestant countries) is blessed with those spiritual hymns, to the frequent use whereof the apostle doth so solemnly exhort.
>
> As a sincere desire to promote divine psalmody has prompted me to this translation; so I presume to address the same, such as it is, to your Royal Highnesses for no other end, than to promote thereby the singing the praises of our blessed Redeemer . . . .
>
> May the Lord Jesus, the great Lover of Souls, prepare your Royal Highnesses tender hearts for so divine an exercise. (iii,iv)

Jacobi makes no distinction between psalmody and hymnody, but since the majority of the poems in the *Psalmodia Germanica* are not psalms, but hymns, Jacobi's stated purpose "to promote divine psalmody" is the same as that of the author of the *Lyra Davidica*.

The German congregations in London were very influential in spreading the practice of hymn singing as a part of the church service, and thereby indirectly stimulated the translation of German hymns. In the preface to *Psalmodia Germanica* (1722) Jacobi states:

> Many of the British nation, having heard the sacred psalmody us'd in the German congregations at London, have wish'd to see the same done into English, and set to the same tunes and metre, wherein they were originally comps'd. To gratify this pious desire, a specimen is publish'd now taken from some thousands of hymns, wherewith the German psalmody abounds.

Jacobi shows very good judgment in his "specimen" of German hymns, and he includes in the *Psalmodia Germanica* many of the very best hymns in the language. Time has also shown approval of his taste, and many of the hymns he selected to translate have become traditional favorites in English. He included some of the best of Luther's hymns including "Aus tieffer Noth schrey ich zu dir," "Ein feste Burg ist unser Gott," and "Komm Heiliger Geist, Herre Gott." Three of Paul Gerhardt's best hymns are translated: "Wach auf mein Hertz und singe," "Wie soll ich dich empfangen," and "Befiehl du deine Wege." Johannes Heermann, whom Julian ranks with "the best of his century" is represented with "Jesu deine heilige Wunden," "O Jesu du mein Bräutigam," and "Treuer Gott ich muss dir klagen." Other important hymns are Johannes Scheffler's "Liebe, die du mich zum Bilde," Martin Rinkart's "Nun dancket alle Gott," and Philip Nicolai's "Wie schön leuchtet der Morgenstern." One of the greatest of the seventeenth century hymns translated by Jacobi is Johann

Rist's powerful "O Ewigkeit du Donnerwort." The first stanza of this hymn is quoted below with Jacobi's translation.

> O Ewigkeit, du Donnerwort!
> O Schwert, das durch die Seele bohrt!
> O Anfang sonder Ende!
> O Ewigkeit, Zeit ohne Zeit:
> Ich weiss für grosser Traurigkeit
> Nicht, wo ich mich hinwende.
> Mein ganz erschrocknes Herz erbebt,
> Daß mir die Zung am Gaumen klebt.

> Eternity! tremendous Word,
> Home-striking point, heart-piercing sword,
> Beginning without ending!
> Eternity! without a shore,
> Where ever fiery billows roar,
> What is thy sight portending?
> One glimpse of thine unfathom'd deep
> Wou'd rouse a wretch from sinful sleep.

Although Jacobi was quite free with his translation, (and the wretch being roused from sinful sleep is a real departure), he retains the meter and rhyme scheme, and on the whole his version seems to carry the cumulative and sustained intensity of Rist's poem that has made it a masterpiece.

One of Paul Gerhardt's greatest hymns, "Wie soll ich dich empfangen," was translated by Jacobi as "How shall I meet my Saviour." The first stanzas are quoted for comparison.

> Wie soll ich dich empfangen?
> Und wie begegn ich dir?
> O aller Welt Verlangen,
> O meiner Seelen Zier,
> O Jesu, Jesu, setze
> Mir selbst die Fackel bei,
> Damit, was dich ergetze,
> Mir kund und wissend sei!

> How shall I meet my Saviour?
> How shall I welcome Thee?
> What manner of behaviour
> Is now requir'd of me?
> Lord, thine illumination
> Set heart and hands aright,
> That this my preparation
> Be pleasing in thy sight.

Jacobi's translation of Martin Rinkart's "Nun danket alle Gott," although lacking the quality of Catherine Winkworth's version, "Now thank we all our God," was popular throughout the eighteenth century and was repeated in the Moravian hymn books from 1754 to 1886.

Nun danket alle Gott
Mit Herzen, Mund und Händen,
Der grosse Dinge thut
An uns und allen Enden,
Der uns von Mutteleib
Und Kindesbeinen an
Unzählig viel zu gut
Und noch jetzund gethan.

Now let us praise the Lord
With body, soul and spirit,
Who doth such wondrous things
Beyond our sense and merit,
Who from our mother's womb
And tender infancy
Preserves our life and limbs
In health and liberty.

Before continuing the history of the translation of German hymns, I should like to point out one of the unusual features of many of these hymns—their meter and rhyme scheme.

Martin Luther had experimented with various meters and rhyme schemes as in his most famous hymn, "Ein feste Burg ist unser Gott." Especially the lines:

Der alt böse Feind
Mit Ernst ers itzt meint,
Gross Macht und viel List
Sein grausam Rüstung ist.

This irregular meter had been taken up somewhat in the English hymn but for the most part the metrical psalms and hymns in England retained the "common meter" which was a four line stanza, the first and third lines consisting of four feet, usually rhyming, and the lines usually "end stopped." This use of the "common meter" was especially prevalent when the lyrics were written expressly for use in worship, as were the psalms. The sixth edition of the "New Version" of the psalms by Tate and Brady printed in the Savoy (1708) used what the authors called "peculiar measures," and "near thirty new tunes." It would be interesting to know if they were familiar with the "peculiar measures" used in the *Lyra Davidica* published the same year. According to Jacobi many of the "new tunes" were German in origin, and many tunes thought to be English that were taken from Henry Playford's *Harmonia Sacra* (1693) were also German in origin.[9]

The use of "peculiar measures" in the "New Version" may have encouraged Isaac Watts to experiment with various meters, although Watts was well acquainted, of course, with all types of poetic meter from sources other than the "New Version" of the psalms. An example of Watts' rare use of "peculiar measure" is in his hymn "Lord of the Worlds Above."

Lord of the worlds above,
How pleasant and how fair
The dwellings of thy love,
Thine earthly temples are!
  To thine abode
  My heart aspires,
  With warm desires
  To see my God.

Far more unusual meter and rhyme patterns were common in German hymnody and were to be found in abundance in the *Lyra Davidica* and in the *Psalmodia Germanica*.

One of the German hymn writers who used unusual meter and rhyme with great success was Joachim Neander (1650?-1680). What was probably his greatest hymn, "Lobe den Herren den mächtigen König der Ehren," did not appear in English translation until 1765 in the *Supplement to German Psalmody* which also contained his evening hymn, "Der Tag ist hin, mein Jesu, bei mir bleibe"—the inspiration for Henry Francis Lyte's famous "Abide with me, fast falls the eventide." In 1720 Jacobi translated Neander's "Grosser Prophete, mein Herze begehret" as "Heavenly prophet, my heart is desiring." In 1722 he translated "Wunderbarer König," and "Meine Hoffnung stehet feste." Since these two hymns are so typical of Neander's use of unusual meter and rhyme, I have quoted the first stanzas of Jacobi's translations below:

Wonderful creator,
Soveraign arbitrator!
Look upon us in thy mercy.
Christ our blessed Saviour,
Slight not our behaviour
Though we have rebell'd against Thee.
Lord our King!
Make us sing,
With a due contrition
And profound submission.

All my hope is fix'd and grounded
In the great and living Lord;
He's my help, when I'm surrounded
Or with pest, with fire, or sword;
  Him alone,
  God or none,
I acknowledge for my own.

Ironically, the hymn writer most strongly attracted to German hymnody, Charles Wesley, published very few hymns that were not in the common meter or regular meter with lengthened lines. This was probably due to the editorial dictatorship exercised by his brother John, who, although himself strongly under the spell of German spiritual influences and hymnody, tried to avoid any of the excesses or irregularities he found in the German hymns. Therefore, Charles' lines:

> O how sweet it is to languish
>> For our God
>> Till his blood
> Eases all our anguish

were not printed in the Methodist hymn books edited by John. Perhaps the closest to an unusual rhyme scheme that passed John's censorship was the hymn by Charles:

> My God I am thine: what comfort divine,
> What a blessing to know that my Jesus is mine!
> In the heavenly Lamb thrice happy I am —
> My heart doth rejoice at the sound of his name.

Charles Wesley's hymn "All praise to the Lamb" also has this meter and rhyme scheme.

One of Jacobi's best translations is of Philip Nicolai's "Wie schön leuchtet der Morgenstern," one of the great German hymns, and one that exhibits the "peculiar" use of meter and rhyme that was so uncommon in English hymns and psalms. An earlier translation of this hymn had appeared in the *Lyra Davidica*. The first stanzas of the original and Jacobi's translation follow:

> Wie schön leuchtet der Morgenstern,
> Voll Gnad und Wahrheit von dem Herrn,
> Die süsse Wurzel Jesse!
> Du Sohn Davids, aus Jacobs Stamm,
> Mein König und mein Bräutigam,
> Hast mir mein Hertz besessen,
> Lieblich, freundlich,
> Schön und herrlich, Gross und ehrlich,
> Reich von Gaben,
> Hoch und sehr prächtig erhaben.

> How bright appears the morning star
> With grace and truth beyond compare,
> The royal root of Jesse!
> O David's Son of Jacob's line!
> My soul's delight and spouse divine,
> Thy love can only bless me.
> Precious, gracious,
> Fair and glorious, e'er victorious
> Thou my treasure
> Art beyond all joy and pleasure.

Johann Christian Jacobi had been the major transmitter of German poetry into England during the 1720s and early 1730s. The writers who now took this place were John and Charles Wesley, who began their hymn publishing career in 1737 with *A Collection of Psalms and Hymns*. This hymn collection marked the beginning of one of the

23

most important cultural and literary links between England and Germany in the eighteenth century. The union of the Wesleys with the German Moravians was not only important for the transmission of further German poetry into England, but was in a large measure responsible for the entire evangelical revival of the eighteenth century and the consequent influence of this revival on English culture and literature. The story of the Wesley-Moravian relationship has been told often, occasionally well. One of the most judicious histories of this relationship has been given by Clifford W. Towlson in his book *Moravian and Methodist*. I shall therefore present only the outline of events and attempt to suggest their significance.

In October 1735, John and Charles Wesley embarked on the *Simonds* for Georgia. John was going as a missionary to the Indians and Charles was going to serve as secretary to Governor Oglethorpe. On board the *Simonds* were twenty-six German Moravians and a group of German Lutheran refugees from Salzburg. Four days before sailing, John wrote in his journal: "I began to learn German, in order to converse with the Moravians." (Oct. 17, 1735) In describing the daily routine of the trip which lasted from October 21, 1735 to January 6, 1736, John wrote: "From nine till twelve I usually learned German.... At seven I joined with the Germans in their public service." (Oct. 21, 1735) The bishop of the Moravians, the elderly David Nitschmann, greatly impressed the young Wesley. David Nitschmann was the cousin of Anna Nitschmann, the second wife of Count Zinzendorf and a prominent hymn writer in her own right. Wesley wrote in his journal about Bishop Nitschmann: "In the afternoon David Nitschmann, bishop of the Moravians, and two others began to learn English. O may we be, not only of one tongue, but of one mind and of one heart!" (Oct. 21, 1735)

The momentous experience during the storm that so impressed the young Wesley has been told and retold, but as Clifford Towlson has wisely said: "The story has such charm that it loses nothing by repetition." It appears in Wesley's journal, October 25, 1735:

> At noon our third storm began. At four it was more violent than any before. Now indeed we could say, The waves of the sea were mighty and raged horribly. They rose up to the heavens above, and clave down to hell beneath. The winds roared round about us, and (what I never heard before) whistled as distinctly as if it had been a human voice. The ship not only rocked to and fro with the utmost violence, but shook and jarred with so unequal, grating a motion, that one could not but with great difficulty keep hold on any thing, nor stand a moment without it. Every ten minutes came a shock against the stern or side of the ship, which one would think should dash the planks in pieces ....
> At seven I went to the Germans. I had long before observed the great seriousness of their behaviour. Of their humility they had given a continual proof, by performing those servile offices for the other passengers, which none of the English would undertake; for which they desired, and would receive no pay, saying, "It was good for their proud hearts," and "Their Loving Saviour had done more for

them." And every day had given them occasion of shewing a meekness which no injury could move. If they were pushed, struck, or thrown down, they rose again and went away; but no complaint was found in their mouth. There was now an opportunity of trying whether they were delivered from the spirit of fear, as well as from that of pride, anger, and revenge. In the midst of the psalm wherewith their service began, the sea broke over, split the main sail in pieces, covered the ship, and poured in between the decks, as if the great deep had already swallowed us up. A terrible screaming began among the English. The Germans calmly sung on. I asked one of them afterwards, "Were you not afraid?" He answered, "I thank God, No." I asked, "But were not your women and children afraid?" He replied mildly, "No; our women and children are not afraid to die." From them I went to their crying trembling neighbours, and pointed out to them the difference, in the hour of trial, between him that feareth God, and him that feareth him not. At twelve the wind fell. This was the most glorious day which I have hitherto seen.

In Georgia the Wesleys became acquainted with the German Bishop August Gottlieb Spangenberg who worked in both America and England for the Moravian organization and who later became their leader at Herrnhut on the death of Zinzendorf. He was also an accomplished hymn writer and John Wesley later translated his "Der König ruht, und schauet doch" into English, making a complimentary reference to the Moravians in the process.

> Devoted to their Common Lord,
> True followers of the Bleeding Lamb;
> By God belov'd, by men abhor'd —
> And Hernhuth is the fav'rite name![10]

It was the Moravian Bishop August Gottlieb Spangenberg who first started Wesley on the road to a belief in salvation through faith and the personal witness of the Spirit. This movement toward Pietism and a personal relationship with Christ is a most important factor in the development of the minds of John and Charles Wesley. It is strongly revealed in their hymns, and subsequently became a part of the general literary movement toward subjectivism and emotionalism in the later eighteenth century. Consequently, this phase of the development of the mind of John Wesley under the influence of the German Moravians is important for a complete understanding of the development of the English Romantic movement. Unfortunately it has been a neglected chapter in the long history of this movement.

Although Wesley had closer connections with the Moravian leaders Peter Böhler and Ludwig Zinzendorf, it was Spangenberg who really started him on the road of introspection. The following is from John Wesley's journal. (Feb. 7, 1736)

> Mr. Oglethorpe returned from Savannah, with Mr. Spangenberg, one of the Pastors of the Germans. I soon found what spirit he was of, and asked his advice with regard to my own conduct. He said, "My brother, I must first ask you one or two questions. Have you the witness within yourself? Does the Spirit of God bear witness with your spirit that you are a child of God?" I was surprised, and knew not what to answer. He observed it and asked, "Do you know Jesus Christ?"

I paused and said, "I know he is the Saviour of the world." "True;" replied he; "but do you know he has saved *you*?" I answered, "I hope he has died to save me." He only added, "Do you know yourself?" I said, "I do," but I fear they were vain words.

Following this interesting conversation Wesley's German interests increased and he attended the meetings of the Moravians as often as possible. Thomas Herbert in his important work on John Wesley has said of Wesley's life in Georgia:

> ...he talked and sang in German; read German books; wrote in German; mastered and reviewed a German grammar and a German dictionary, then transcribed them to fix their contents in his memory; and, finally he wrote a German grammar and compiled a German dictionary of his own. From this time until 1740, he was almost continuously in contact and communication with German-speaking people.[11]

Until 1882 Wesley biographers did not understand Wesley's statement that he had published a book of hymns in 1736. This was while Wesley was in America and the first of the Wesley hymns were thought to have been published in London in 1738. In 1882 there was found in a London book store a volume containing seventy-eight hymns entitled: *Collection of Psalms and Hymns*, Charles-Town, printed by Lewis Timothy, 1737. Although no author is mentioned this book of hymns is now known to be by John Wesley, and the book represents his first attempt at translation from German for publication. In the book are five hymns with the inscription "from the German." As Clifford Towlson has correctly pointed out, this is a small number compared with the thirty-one hymns from Isaac Watts included in the collection. It is likely that even at this early date John Wesley was adhering to the principal of careful selection he later explained in his journal:

> I translated many of their hymns, for the use of our own congregations. Indeed as I durst not implicitly follow any man, I did not take all that lay before me, but selected those which I judged to be most scriptural and most suitable to sound experience.

John Wesley was always the more pragmatic of the brothers, and certainly adhered to the motto that has often been associated with his friend Dr. Johnson: "no nonsense." John loved William Law in spite of his mystical leanings while others loved him because of them. It was this element in John's nature that caused him to reject many of the emotional hymns so prevalent in German hymnody, and especially did he reject the expressions of too personal a familiarity with the Savior. Charles Wesley's most beloved hymn. "Jesus lover of my soul," which breathed too much of the spirit of German emotionalism, found no place in the large Methodist hymn books edited by John.

John Wesley's care in selecting German hymns for translation was by no means a deterrent to the reception of German poetry in England.

26

On the contrary, his conforming to more restrained English tastes and his skill as a translator greatly stimulated English interest in this branch of German literature.

> Wesley adopted this policy of careful selection by including only five German hymns in his Charlestown collection . . . one of which is perhaps the best of them all, "Thou hidden love of God," his great version of Tersteegen's "Verborgene Gottesliebe du," a translation which Emerson declared to be the greatest hymn in the English language. (Towlson, 202)

Since it is Charles who has been considered the better hymn writer of the two brothers, it seems appropriate to the purposes of this study to include here the translation by John that Ralph Waldo Emerson has declared to be "the greatest hymn in the English language." The hymn has a progressive development typical of many German hymns: from desires for God and a feeling of separation, through striving and searching, to an eventual union in love.

> Thou hidden love of God, whose height,
> Whose depth unfathomed, no man knows,
> I see from far thy beauteous light,
> Inly I sigh for thy repose:
> My heart is pained, nor can it be
> At rest, till it finds rest in thee.
>
> Thy secret voice invites me still
> The sweetness of thy yoke to prove;
> And fain I would; but though my will
> Seem fixed, yet wide my passions rove;
> Yet hind'rances strew all the way;
> I aim at thee, yet from thee stray.
>
> Tis mercy all that thou has brought
> My mind to seek, her peace in thee!
> Yet while I seek, but find thee not,
> No peace my wand'ring soul shall see:
> O when shall all my wand'rings end,
> And all my steps to thee-ward tend!
>
> Is there a thing beneath the sun
> That strives with thee my heart to share?
> Ah, tear it thence, and reign alone,
> The lord of every motion there!
> Then shall my heart from earth be free,
> When it hath found repose in thee.
>
> O hide this self from me, that I
> No more, but Christ in me, may live!
> My vile affections crucify,
> Nor let one darling lust survive!
> In all things nothing may I see,
> Nothing desire or seek, but thee!
>
> O Love, thy sovereign aid impart,
> To save me from low-thoughted care;
> Chase this self-will through all my heart,

Through all its latent mazes there:
Make me thy duteous child, that I
Ceaseless may Abba, Father, cry.

Ah no! ne'er will I backward turn;
Thine wholly, thine alone, I am!
Thrice happily he who views with scorn
Earth's joys, for thee his constant flame:
O help, that I may never move
From the blest footsteps of thy love!

Each moment draws from earth away
My heart, that lowly waits thy call;
Speak to my inmost soul, and say,
"I am thy Love, thy God, thy All!"
To feel thy power, to hear thy voice
To taste thy love, be all my choice.

Clifford Towlson suggests that "one hymn by Johann Andreas Rothe
. . . can challenge Tersteegen's famous hymn for the fame of being
the greatest hymn ever written. 'Ich habe nun den Grund gefunden'
is a magnificent hymn of faith in adversity which Wesley has made
even more magnificent in 'Now I have found the ground'". (Towlson,
202) I quote below three stanzas of this hymn, the last of which is
interesting in its imagery because of the experience Wesley had
aboard the ship *Simonds* with the Moravians, but I think it must be
admitted that Tersteegen's "Verborgene Gottesliebe du" is a superior
hymn, primarily because of its progressive movement of desire for
God, searching, and final union.

Now I have found the ground wherein
Sure my soul's anchor may remain;
The wounds of Jesus — for my sin
Before the world's foundation slain,
Whose mercy shall unshaken stay,
When heaven and earth are fled away.

O love, thou bottomless abyss!
My sins are swallowed up in thee;
Covered is my unrighteousness,
Nor spot of guilt remains on me,
While Jesus' blood, through earth and skies,
Mercy, free boundless mercy, cries!

Though waves and storms go o'er my head,
Though strength, and health, and friends be gone,
Though joys be withered all and dead,
Though every comfort be withdrawn,
On this my steadfast soul relies,
Father, thy mercy never dies.

In assessing the importance of Wesley's relationship with theMora-
vians, it can be said that he learned the importance of hymn-singing

from them and discovered through them the great wealth of German lyric poetry.

> It was the sublime achievement of the Moravians that they introduced him, and through him thousands of his followers, to the beauty, the dignity, the reverence, the fitness of the German chorale, and to the personal and intimate song of the great Pietists. (Towlson, 195)

> ... but for the voyage to Georgia and the contacts with the Moravians on the *Simonds* and in America, Wesley would not have made his wonderful translations, without which English hymnody would have been incalculably the poorer. (Towlson, 201)

As has been indicated, John Wesley's translations did not end with the five hymns in the Charlestown hymn book, nor did his connections with the German Moravians end in Georgia. In 1738 he returned to England and in his journal he writes under the date of 7 Feb., 1738:

> Tuesday 7, (a day much to be remembered,) at the house of Mr. Weinantz, a Dutch merchant, I met Peter Bohler [sic], Schulius Richter, [Julius], and Wensel Neiser, just then landed from Germany. Finding they had no acquaintance in England, I offered to procure them a lodging, and did so near Mr. Hutton's where I then was. And from this time I did not wilingly lose any opportunity of conversing with them, while I stayed in London.

Under the constant instruction of Peter Böhler, who cultivated the seed planted by Spangenberg in Georgia, John Wesley began to accept the Pietist doctrine of salvation by faith, which led finally to the turning experience in his life, the meeting at Aldersgate street on 24 May, 1738. From his journal:

> In the evening, I went very unwillingly to a Society in Aldersgatestreet, where one was reading Luther's Preface to the Epistle to the Romans. About a quarter before nine, while he was describing the change which God works in the heart through faith in Christ, I felt my heart strangely warmed. I felt I did trust in Christ; Christ alone, for salvation; and an assurance was given me, that he had taken away *my* sins, even *mine*, and saved *me* from the law of sin and death.

Charles Wesley was going through the same experience of conversion under the teaching of Peter Böhler, and the importance of this concept of salvation by faith and of Jesus as one's *personal* Savior cannot be over emphasized, either as a contribution to the general cultural pattern out of which literature grows, or as a direct contribution to the subjective and emotional trend that soon permeated the spiritual lyric poetry in England as it had done in Germany. John Wesley wrote in his journal: "Peter Bohler left London in order to embark for Carolina. O what a work has God begun, since his coming into England! Such an one as shall never come to an end, till heaven and earth pass away." (4 May, 1738)

After these experiences with Peter Böhler, John Wesley had a great desire to go to Germany, and especially to Herrnhut, "to see the

29

place where the Christians live," and he did so in June, 1738. He renewed his acquaintance with Count Zinzendorf whom he had met in England, he met Peter Böhler's father, renewed his acquaintance with David Nitschmann, and met many other important men involved in the Moravian movement. He also went to Halle where he met "Professor Francke, who behaved with utmost humanity," and thus Wesley made personal contact with the two major Pietist movements in Germany.[12] He returned to England September 17, 1738.

After his return to London he published *A Collection of Psalms and Hymns* which contained five new translations from the German added to the five translations from the 1737 volume, making a total of ten German hymns. In 1739 he published *Hymns and Sacred Poems* jointly with Charles, and this volume contained the ten hymns translated earlier and twelve new translations. This volume of hymns was very popular and went through three editions before the end of the year. In 1740 John and Charles published another collection with the title *Hymns and Sacred Poems* which contained six new translations from the German. In 1742 John published twenty-four of his translations in *A Collection of German Hymns*. In all, as far as can be determined, John Wesley translated thirty-six hymns from German. In the "Supplement" I have listed the most important collections in which these hymns were published in the eighteenth century to 1770, but I have not attempted to trace them into the numerous collections of later publishers and editors. James Taft Hatfield writing in 1896 has the following to say in regard to the general dispersion of these German hymns.

> The translations are not only used throughout the wide circle of Methodist ad-
> herents, but I find them in not less than 100 important collections, including all
> phases of religious confession, with the exception, as far as I have found, of the
> Roman Catholic. Outside of the Methodist group, the Church of England has
> made use of them in the hymnals of Madan, Kennedy, Maurice, Bickersteth, and
> Thring; in the Sarum, Westminister Abbey, and Rugby hymn-books; in the widely
> used publications of the Society for the Propagation of Christian Knowledge; in
> the Churchman's Altar Manual, and many other collections; they are represented
> in the standard and special collections of the American Episcopalian, the Baptist,
> Moravian, Congregational, Swedenborgian, Lutheran, and Dutch Reformed
> churches; they occur, I believe, in all standard Unitarian collections. In many
> English collections in the first half of this century they are published anonymously
> or from false sources, as in those of Rippon, Montgomery, and Bikersteth.[13]

It is interesting to note that John and Charles Wesley were attracted to German music as well as to the lyrics. In 1742 they published a *Collection of Thirty-six tunes, set to music, as they are commonly sung at the Foundry*. (The Methodists were then using a vacated foundry as a meeting place). This book contains forty-two tunes, thirteen of which are German hymn tunes, and one other tune is taken from Handel's opera *Riccardo Primo*. Many of the tunes used by Wesley were taken from the 1704 or the 1714 edition of Johann Freylinghausen's *Geist-reiches Gesang-Buch*. The former (1704) contained 683 hymns and 173 melodies, and the latter (1714) contained 815 hymns and 154 melodies. There are two copies of Freylinghausen's *Geist-reiches Gesang-Buch* in the library of Richmond College, both initialled "J.W." (Towlson, 204). Freylinghausen was the son-in-law of August Hermann Francke, the leader of Halle Pietism, and Francke's successor at Halle on the latter's death in 1727. "As a hymn-writer Freylinghausen" according to Julian, "ranks not only as the best of the Pietistic school, but as the first among his contemporaries." (396)

John Wesley also translated two of Freylinghausen's hymns: "Monarche aller Ding" as "Monarch of all, with lowly fear," in *Hymns and Sacred Poems* (1739), and "Wer ist wohl wie du," as "O Jesu, source of calm repose," in *Psalms and Hymns* (1737). Julian calls this last hymn by Freylinghausen "one of his noblest and most beautiful hymns, a mirror of his inner life, and one of the finest of the German 'Jesus hymns'." The *Collection of ... Tunes* also reveals that Wesley was familiar with Jacobi's *Psalmodia Germanica* since three of the melodies used in Wesley's *Collection* were taken from Jacobi's work.

One of the most interesting connections the Wesleys had with German music was through the acquaintance of Johann Friedrich Lampe, the collaborator with Henry Carey in ballad operas. In 1746 Charles Wesley published his *Hymns on the Great Festivals and other Occasions* and Johann Lampe had assisted in this publication by composing the music. "These tunes," according to the *Dictionary of National Biography* "insured for [Charles Wesley's] hymns a long term of popularity." On Lampe's death Charles Wesley wrote a hymn in his honor beginning "Tis done, the sov'reign Will's obeyed."

The question of the "influence" of German hymnody on the Wesleys and the subsequent result of this "influence" on other English writers and on English literature in general is difficult to answer in definite terms, as I have suggested in the introduction to this chapter. There was certainly a stimulation from the German hymns which to a large extent changed the direction of spiritual poetry in England.

> The influence of Moravian hymnody over the Wesleys was not primarily concerned, however, with the knowledge of hymn-tunes which the Methodist leader thus acquired, nor even with his monumental translations, but in a new conception of the function and power of sacred song. What had formerly been to the Wesleys a means of worship, an approach to God, on the part of the believer, now became a medium by which the unbeliever might find salvation. (Towlson, 206)

German hymnody did not acquaint the Wesleys with something they had never known, but German hymnody did change their attitude toward the function and power of the hymn. It was not so much an innovation as an enriching and a broadening of an established heritage.

Following the movement begun by the Wesleys, the hymn was no longer the property of a few dissenting groups in England. It was introduced into nearly every major religious body as an integral part of worship, including the Church of England. Many hymn writers followed the example of John and Charles Wesley by turning to the long tradition of spiritual poetry in Germany as a source of inspiration. Some of the more important hymn writers who also translated from the German were: the popular Baptist minister Benjamin Beddome; Wesley's friend and member of the "Holy Club" John Gambold; the author of "Rock of Ages", Augustus M. Toplady; and some lesser known translators including William Delamotte, a friend and convert of Charles Wesley; Charles Kinchen, another friend of Charles Wesley; and the Reverend L. T. Nyberg. Many of these hymn writers also had direct connections with the German Moravians in England and in Germany, and John Gambold actually became a Bishop of the Moravian church in England. There were also Germans who translated hymns into English, among them Philip Heinrich Molther and Ernst Ludolf Schlicht.

Of course, being inspired or stimulated by German spiritual poetry does not in itself produce great literature, as John Wesley so aptly stated in the preface to his hymn book of 1780.

> I desire men of taste to judge whether there is not in some of the following verses the true Spirit of Poetry; such as cannot be acquired by art and labour; but must be the gift of nature. By labour a man may become a tolerable imitator of Spenser or Shakespeare or Milton and may heap together pretty compound epithets as "pale eyed," Weak eyed" and the like. But unless he is born a poet he will never attain to genuine Spirit of poetry.

These statements about "the gift of nature," "Spirit of poetry," and Wesley's attitude against the art of imitation are quite revealing of the critical attitudes of John Wesley and the close afinity of these critical attitudes with the general literary and critical atmosphere of the time.

The importance of Methodism and the religious revival to the cultural and literary pattern in the later eighteenth century has been discussed by a number of writers.[14] One aspect of this revival, however, which needs to be reemphasized is the personal, subjective mood of John and Charles Wesley's hymns which had its source in German Pietism and found its culmination in English Romanticism.

One of the most obvious elements of German spiritual poetry is its extremly personal and subjective nature. While Luther wrote "Ein feste Burg ist *unser* Gott," Paul Gerhardt, one of the major contributors to this personal atmosphere in spiritual poetry, wrote "Erkenne *mich, mein* Hüter! *Mein* Hirte, nimm *mich* an." The element of mysticism that pervaded the culture of seventeenth-century Germany and the Pietistic element in the late seventeenth and early eighteenth centuries were strong factors in this intensely personal love for Christ. In Paul Gerhardt's famous hymn, "O Haupt voll Blut und Wunden," which was translated by John Gambold in 1754, some form of "ich," "mich," or "mein" appears in over half of the eighty lines. The same can be said of Gerhardt's hymn "O Jesu Christ, mein schönstes Licht." This hymn was translated by John Wesley in 1739 and appeared in collections other than the Wesley's in various forms in 1746, 1754, and 1765. The first two stanzas of Wesley's translation follow. (italics mine)

> Jesus, thy boundless love to *me*
> No thought can reach, no tongue declare:
> O knit *my* thankful heart to thee,
> And reign without a rival there!
> *Thine wholly, thine alone, I am*;
> Be thou alone *my* constant flame.
>
> O grant that nothing in *my* soul
> May dwell, but thy pure love alone!
> *O may thy love possess me whole,*
> *My* joy, *my* treasure, and *my* crown!
> Strange flames far from *my* heart remove,
> *My* every act, word, thought be love.

The German mystic and poet Johannes Scheffler (Anglus Silesius) was another contributor to this imagery of personal relationship with Christ. As a writer of spiritual poems he certainly deserves to be classed with the very best of Germany's long list of lyric poets. For beautiful imagery and intensity of feeling he is hardly surpassed, and these qualities were not overlooked by hymn writers in England in the eighteenth century. No less than ten of his moving spiritual poems were translated in the first half of the century. One of his greatest, "Liebe, die du mich zum Bilde," that Julian calls "one of the most beautiful and profound hymns of the spiritual love of the soul to her Saviour" (674) was translated by Jacobi in 1720 as "Lord thine image thou hast lent me." Julian says this is one of Jacobi's best translations and this judgment seems to be substantiated by the fact that his translation was published again in 1725 and 1732, in the Moravian hymn book of 1754, and in Lady Huntingdon's collection of 1780. Julian gives an interesting anecdote concerning this hymn.

> ... one evening in 1722 Benjamin Schultze, a German missionary at Madras, sang it from Freylinghausen, and was so delighted with it that he determined that his Malabar scholars should share his pleasure. That evening he translated verse after verse, not resting till he had finished it two hours after midnight. The success he attained led him to translate 103 hymns from the German which are still sung in South India. (164)

Here is the first stanza of this poem that had such a powerful effect on its readers.

Liebe, die du mich zum Bilde
Deiner Gottheit hast gemacht,
Liebe, die du mich so milde
Nach dem Fall hast wieder bracht.
Liebe, dir ergeb ich mich
Dein zu bleiben ewiglich.

Of the many translations of the hymns of Johannes Scheffler in the
early eighteenth century, four were by John Wesley, and it is in these
hymns that we find a strong movement toward the subjective and
personal element that so pervaded the German spiritual poetry of the
seventeenth century. John Wesley's poem "O God, of good the
unfathom'd sea" is what John Julian calls "a vigorous and full ren-
dering of Scheffler's poem 'Du unvergleichlichs Gut'." This poem is
a masterpiece of balance and sustained thought. The dynamics of the
poem are from a general love of God to an expression of personal
love of God and a desire for the "unio mystica" of which Scheffler
speaks so often. Stanza one expresses the universal desire for God
by using the impersonal "wer".

Du unvergleichlichs Gut, wer wollte dich nicht lieben?
Wer wollte nicht sein Herz um dich, o Gott, betrüben?
Wer wollte nicht mit Geist und Sinn
In dich, mein Jesu, wandern hin?

In translating this poem, John Wesley must have felt something of an
ambivalence as he attempted to retain the spirit of nearness to the
Savior without including a suggestion of the "unio mystica." He
does not translate the last line with the imagery of a union with
Christ, and to make sure that this love of Jesus is of a general nature he
adds the line "O Jesus, Lover of Mankind!"

O God, of good th' unfathomed sea!
Who would not give his heart to thee?
Who would not love thee with his might?
O Jesus, Lover of mankind!
Who would not his whole soul and mind,
With all his strength, to Thee unite?

The six stanzas following this introduction are each made up of a two
line address to God stating respectively his grandeur, majesty, wisdom,
goodness, beauty, and power, and the concluding two lines of each
stanza express in striking contrast the "creaturliness" of man and the
mercy and goodness of God in that he concerns himself with man.
Stanza three:

Du bist die Majestät, der alles Ehr erzeiget,
Den Herr, vor dem Erd, Höll und Himmel tief sich neiget.
Und doch neigst du dich, Herr, so weit
Zu mir, der schnödsten Schnödigkeit.

34

And John Wesley's translation:

> Astonished at thy frowning brow,
> Earth, hell, and heaven's strong pillars bow:
> Terrible majesty is thine!
> Who then can that vast love express,
> Which bows thee down to me, who less
> Than nothing am, till Thou art mine!

In the final stanza Scheffler completes the transition from a general love of God to a personal love of God. He does this by a variation of the first stanza in which the "wer wollte dich nicht lieben" becomes "wie sollt *ich* dich nicht lieben."

> O unvergleichlichs Gut, wie sollt ich dich nicht lieben?
> Wie sollte sich mein Herz nach dir nicht stets betrüben?
> Ach wäre doch mein Geist und Sinn
> In dich schon ganz, mein Jesu, hin.

Wesley failed to make this progression to a stronger bond of personal love and longing for Jesus in the last stanza, and instead he repeated the first stanza word for word.

John Wesley was, however, not at all consistent in his avoidance of terms of familiarity with deity, and he retained such expressions in his translations as long as he felt the image of intimacy with Jesus was on a high spiritual level. He feared any exaggerated expression of mysticism and this fear nearly caused a serious rift between himself and his earliest spiritual guide, William Law. From Wesley's journal:

> In riding to Bradford, I read over Mr. Law's book on the New Birth: philosophical, speculative, precarious; Behmenish [containing the philosophy of Jacob Böhme], void, and vain! Oh what a fall is there!

But he is not always sure where mysticism ends end where pure love of Christ begins. His translation of Scheffler's "Ich will dich lieben, meine Stärke" is quite literal and very florid:

> Thee will I love, my strength, my tower:
> Thee will I love, my joy, my crown;
> Thee will I love with all my power,
> In all thy works, and thee alone;
> Thee will I love, till the pure fire
> Fills my whole soul with chaste desire.

It is interesting to note that in translating this poem filled with such passionate love, John decided not to translate the second stanza which evidently goes too far in its enthusiastic expression of love:

> Ich will dich lieben, Gottes Lamm,
> Als meinen Bräutigam.

The personal element that is so strong in the spiritual poetry of this time and that is also prevalent in the Romantic poetry to follow is very closely related to these uninhibited outpourings of love as exemplified in Scheffler's poem "Ich will dich lieben, meine Stärke." Charles Wesley's character and personality absorbed much more of this atmosphere than did John's, and perhaps that is one reason why Charles is remembered as the poet while John is remembered as the organizer and leader. The inhibitions that restrained John from making reference to Jesus as his Bridegroom did not bother Charles.

> My only care, delight, and bliss,
> My joy, my heaven on earth, be this,
> To hear the Bridegroom's voice!

Although John Wesley refrained from such imagery, he did have an emotional strain that could burst forth on occasions and express his absorption in love. Often these images concern themselves with the infinite magnitude of love and the desire to be all absorbed by this infinity. From J. A. Rothe's "Ich habe nun den Grund gefunden," John translates:

> O love, thou bottomless abyss!
> My sins are swallowed up in thee
>   . . . .
> By faith I plunge me in this sea.

And from Tersteegen's "Verborgne Gottes-Liebe du" he translated:

> Thou hidden love of God, whose height
> Whose depth unfathomed, no man knows,
> Speak to my inmost soul and say,
> "I am thy Love, thy God, thy All."
> To feel thy power, to hear thy voice
> To taste thy Love, be all my choice.

Combined with this desire for absorption in the unfathomed love of God is often a passionate outcry of helplessness. It is easy to imagine these expressions of love as coming from one of the later Romantic poets though in a secularized setting.

An example of this striving and helplessness that brings Shelley to mind is Wesley's translation of S. G. Gmelin's "Ach treib aus meiner Seel." Stanza three reads:

> With outstretched hands and streaming eyes,
> Oft I begin to grasp the prize;
> I groan, I strive, I watch, I pray;
> But ah! how soon it dies away!

One of the most beautiful poems expressing this outcry of helplessness before the "unfathomable depths" combined with a longing for love and absorption in these depths is John Wesley's translation of Ernst Lange's "O Gott, du tieffe sonder Grund." I quote the first three

36

stanzas, which are strongly reminiscent of the lines from J. A. Rothe's "O love, thou bottomless abyss" quoted above.

> O God, thou bottomless abyss!
> Thee to perfection who can know?
> O height immense! What words suffice
> Thy countless attributes to show?
>
> Unfathomable depths thou art!
> O plunge me in thy mercy's sea!
> Void of true wisdom is my heart:
> With love embrace and cover me!
>
> While thee, all infinite I set,
> By faith, before my ravished eye,
> My weakness bends beneath the weight:
> O'erpowered, I sink, I faint, I die.

It is interesting to compare these lines translated by John Wesley with some of Charles Wesley's lines to observe the striking parallel in the emotional expressions of unfathomable love of God and the passionate desire for absorption in this love. The following poem by Charles, sometimes called "Panting for the love of Jesus" is in mood and imagery a companion to the translations by John that have been quoted.

> O Love Divine, how sweet thou art!
> When shall I find my willing heart
> All taken up by thee?
> I thirst, I faint, I die to prove
> The greatness of redeeming love,
> The love of Christ to me.
>   . . . .
> God only knows the love of God:
> O that it now were shed abroad
> In this poor stony heart!
> For love I sigh, for love I pine:
> This only portion, Lord, be mine!
> Be mine this better part!
>   . . . .
> Thy only love do I require,
> Nothing in earth beneath desire,
> Nothing in heaven above:
> Let earth and heaven, and all things go,
> Give me thy only love to know,
> Give me thy only love.

With other words substituted for "Christ," "God," and Lord," this poem could easily become a secular love poem, and in fact very similar images and expressions were used by Shelley.

Shelley was undoubtedly absorbed in this emotional atmosphere of hymnody and at times it seems that he transferred images directly from their spiritual setting in a hymn to a secular setting in one of his poems. Compare, for example, the following expressions of helplessness before all-powerful Love, from John Wesley's translation of Ernst Lange's "O Gott, du tieffe sonder Grund" and Shelley's "Indian Serenade."

Wesley:

> With love embrace and cover me!
>
> . . . .
>
> My weakness bends beneath the weight:
> O'erpowered, I sink, I fant, I die.

Shelley:

> O lift me from the grass!
> I die! I faint! I fail!
> Let thy love in kisses rain
> On my lips and eyelids pale.

Compare also the lines from Charles Wesley's "O Love Divine, how sweet Thou Art," with the fragment by Shelley, "I faint, I perish with my Love."

Wesley:

> I thirst, I faint, I die to prove
> The greatness of redeeming love,
> The love of Christ to me.

Shelley:

> I faint, I perish with my love! I grow
> Frail as a cloud whose (splendors) pale
> Under the evening's ever-changing glow:
> I die like mist upon the gale,
> And like a wave under the calm I fail.

This emotional imagery indicates the extent to which Shelley's poetic mind was absorbing the German and English spiritual poetry, turning this imagery to secular poetry. One of the most marvelous examples of this secularization of the hymn is Shelley's "Hymn to Intellectual Beauty." There have been various attempts to explain this magnificent poetry of Shelley's as something other than what Shelley tells us it is, a hymn. But by comparing the structure of Shelley's hymn with the hymns of John and Charles Wesley it becomes quite obvious that Shelley's "Intellectual Beauty" is a purely lyrical expression of love to a divine power as are the hymns of John and Charles in which they express their love for God and Christ. Obviously, Shelley's "Hymn to Intellectual Beauty" was not so named unintentionally. In many ways its progressive structure is similar to any number of hymns written or translated by the Wesleys, but where their hymns are directed to "the hidden love of God," Shelley's hymn addresses the "awful shadow of some unseen Power," and Charles Wesley's

"Love Divine," is with Shelley a "Spirit of Beauty." The configuration of Shelley's hymn is strikingly parallel to the configuration of Tersteegen's "Verborgene Gottesliebe du," and the fact that Emerson considered John Wesley's translation of this hymn "the greatest hymn in the English language" indicates the esteem in which it was held in intellectual circles. I have said that the progressive structure of Shelley's "Hymn to Intellectual Beauty" is similar to a number of spiritual hymns. This is simply because the lines of development in so many hymns follow a similar pattern and this is especially true in those German hymns that have a tendency toward mysticism. The usual configuration is: 1. separation from God and a desire for union; 2. searching and seeking; 3. recognition of one's unworthiness and plea for mercy; 4. declaration of dedication to God and abdication from the world; 5. the final union with God through love. This is also the progressive configuration of Shelley's "Hymn to Intellectual Beauty." Compare the following lines from Tersteegen's "Verborgene Gottesliebe du" with the lines from Shelley's "Hymn to Intellectual Beauty" as illustrative of this common configurative pattern which I have outlined. The Roman numeral indicates the stanza from which the lines were taken.

1. Statement of the distant intangible object of desire:

    I.   Thou hidden love of God whose height,
            Whose depth unfathomed, no man knows,
            I see from far thy beauteous light

    I.   The awful shadow of some unseen Power
            Floats though unseen among us — visiting
            This various world with as inconstant wing
            As summer winds that creep from flower to flower

2. The beauty of the object expressed; further separation:

    II.   Thy secret voice invites me still
            The sweetness of thy yoke to prove;
               . . . .
            I aim at thee, yet from thee stray.

    II.   Spirit of Beauty, that dost consecrate
            With thine own hues all thou dost shine upon
            Of human thought or form, — where art thou gone?

3. The vanity of mortal aspirations; the desire for freedom through union.

    IV.   Is there a thing beneath the sun
            That strives with thee my heart to share?
            Ah, tear it thence . . .
            Then shall my heart from earth be free,
            When it hath found repose in thee.

    IV.   Love, Hope, and Self-esteem, like clouds depart
            And come, for some uncertain moments lent.
             . . . .

> Thou—that to human thought art nourishment...
> Depart not—lest the grave should be,
> Like life and fear, a dark reality.

4. Turning from past immaturity; coming to truth:

> V.   My vile affections crucify,
> Nor let one darling lust survive!
> In all things nothing may I see,
> Nothing desire or seek, but thee!

> V.   While yet a boy I sought for ghosts, and sped
> Through many a listening chamber, cave and ruin,
>
>   . . . .
>
> I was not heard—I saw them not—
>
>   . . . .
>
> Sudden, thy shadow fell on me;
> I shrieked, and clasped my hands in ecstasy!

5. Dedication and determination; hope:

> VII.   Ah no! ne'er will I backward turn;
> Thine wholly, thine alone, I am!
> Thrice happy he who views with scorn
> Earth's joys, for thee his constant flame.

> VI.   I vowed that I would dedicate my powers
> To thee and thine—have I not kept the vow?
>
>   . . . .
>
> They know that never joy illumed my brow
> Unlinked with hope that thou wouldst free
> This world from its dark slavery.

6. Movement toward union; love:

> VIII.   Each moment draws from earth away
> My heart, that lowly waits thy call;
> Speak to my inmost soul, and say,
> "I am thy Love, thy God, thy All."
> To feel thy power, to hear thy voice,
> To taste thy love, be all my choice.

> VII.   Thus let thy power...
> ... to my onward life supply
> Its calm—to one who worships thee,
> And every form containing thee,
> Whom, Spirit fair, thy spells did bind
> To fear himself, and love all human kind.

The conscious or unconscious means by which Shelley approached and achieved this configurative structure of German spiritual poetry is not the most significant bit of information for this particular study.[15] The configuration itself, however, is evident in many German hymns expressing a mystical love for an unseen power, and the presence of this same configuration in Shelley's hymn adds a new depth of understanding and beauty to one of the most marvellous expressions of English Romantic poetry.

In the history of English literature, the revival of the personal lyric toward the end of the eighteenth century is one of the most fascinating chapters. The secularization of the spiritual lyric as an important part of this chapter has been but suggested here, but is deserving of a much more thorough and extensive treatment.

To conclude this history of the translation and reception of the German hymn there are other names that should be mentioned. John Gambold had been a member of the "Holy Club" at Oxford and in association with the Wesleys he had even been strongly attracted to German mysticism, but, like John, he seems to have lost this form of enthusiasm. At least John Wesley said of him after his return from America: "We [John Wesley and Peter Böhler] went to Stanton Harcourt, to Mr. Gambold, and found my old friend recovered from his *mystic* delusion, and convinced that St. Paul was a better writer than either Tauler or Jacob Behmen." (Journal, 18 Feb., 1738) John Gambold was soon interpreting Böhler's Latin lectures at Oxford and a year later (1739) he became a good friend of Count Zinzendorf and interpreted his German lectures at Oxford.[16] In 1741 John Gambold formally joined the Moravian Brethren, and in 1754 he performed double service for them by becoming the first English Bishop of the *Unitas Fratrum* and by editing the large collection of hymns that became known as the *Moravian hymn-book*. This hymn book was published in two parts. Part one contained 695 hymns, and part two, "containing hymns of the present congregation of the Brethren," contained 460 hymns and several single stanzas. This collection contained translations from the German by both Jacobi and John Wesley, as well as hymns by many other translators. John Gambold included twenty-six translations of his own as well as eighteen original poems. There had been publications of hymns used by the Brethren before 1754, many of them translations, but they were all the work of individuals without the official sanction of the Church. The 1754 edition by Gambold had the sanction of the Church and became the official hymn collection for the English-speaking members.

The man most responsible for the various collections of translations prior to the 1754 edition by Gambold was James Hutton who, like Gambold, had been a close friend of the Wesleys. It was Charles Wesley who introduced Hutton to Count Zinzendorf, and John Wesley introduced him to Peter Böhler. In May of 1738 John Wesley and Peter Böhler had cooperated in organizing a religious society that became the major organizational basis for both the English Moravians and the Methodists. This religious society first met in the home of James Hutton, and in 1739, when the Methodists and Moravians began moving apart, James Hutton and John Gambold moved with the Moravians.[17] Hutton had been operating a bookshop, and after a trip to Germany in 1739 he became the official publisher and distributor of Moravian books and tracts. It is in this capacity that he made his contribution to English hymnody. He was the main editor of the hymn book entitled: *A collection of Hymns, with several translations from the Hymn-book of the Moravian Brethren* (London, 1742). This collection contained 187 hymns and it was continued and expanded through various editions until the official collection of 1754 was published, by which time Hutton's editions had presented over 550 hymns. Many of these hymns passed into the large collection of John Gambold in 1754 and many went into private collections and anthologies. Perhaps the most famous of these private collections were those published by Martin Madan and by the Countess of Huntingdon.

The translation of German spiritual poetry was by no means concluded in the eighteenth century. On the contrary, the many translations dating from the *Lyra Davidica* in 1708 to the *Collection of hymns sung in the Countess of Huntingdon's Chapel* in 1765 mark but an introduction to the reception of German poetry in England. James Montgomery, who ranks with Isaac Watts, Charles Wesley, and William Cowper as a hymn-writer, and who also has a name among writers of non-religious verse, was the son of a Moravian minister, and in 1849 he edited the *Liturgy and Hymns for the use of the Protestant Church of the United Brethren*. Frances Cox gained a reputation in the nineteenth century as an accomplished poet through her *Hymns from the German* (1841 and 1864). One of the greatest translators of all was Catherine Winkworth who published some of the most beautiful translations in her *Lyra Germanica* (1855 to 1858), and in her *Chorale Book for England* (1863). She also contributed to the knowledge of german spiritual poetry with a biographical work, *Christian Singers of Germany* (1869). These are but three of the many writers who followed the tradition of Johann Christian Jacobi and John Wesley. The complete story has never been told.

CONCLUSION

Advocates of Deism in the early eighteenth century, insisting on a religion that was literally universal, "not mysterious," and "as old as the creation," were suddenly confronted with German Pietists, mystics and Moravians, who insisted that religion was personal, mysterious, and that it must be born anew in each individual soul. The German Moravians led by Count Zinzendorf and emphasizing personal salvation and instantaneous conversion found a practical patron in John Wesley, who, seeing the spiritual strength of the Moravian movement without being emotionally overwhelmed by it, carried this movement to its climax in the "Great Awakening," a major factor in providing the emotional and subjective atmosphere for Romanticism. The spiritual lyric, the most subjective of all literary forms, and the literary form most abundantly imported from Germany by the Wesleys and others, gave this "awakening" its dynamics. Both Dryden and Pope expressed their religious sentiments in poetic from, but neither wrote anything quite like William Cowper's

> There is a fountain filled with blood
> Drawn from Emmanuel's veins;
> And sinners, plunged beneath that flood,
> Lose all their guilty stains.
>
> The dying thief rejoiced to see
> That fountain in his day;
> And there have I, as vile as he,
> Washed all my sins away.

In the short time between Pope's *Essay on Man* and Cowper's *Olney Hymns*, 1734-1755, a religious atmosphere had arisen that was antithetic to the rationalism and Deism of the earlier part of the century. The Moravian Peter Böhler had taught John Wesley the necessity of a spiritual conversion and this conversion had nothing in common with "natural" or "rational" religion. William Cowper was a child of this "Great Awakening" and his experience of conversion fits precisely into the pattern that Peter Böhler had outlined for John Wesley. Each individual must find his own way to God, and he can only know that he has found the way through a personal communion with the Spirit. What a reversal from John Toland's *Christianity not Mysterious*. And the literature reflected this reversal. Consider, for example, the effect the religious enthusiasm that produced the following statement might have on any poetry written by the same author:

> Immediately I received strength to believe, and the full beams of the Sun's righteousness shone upon me. I saw the sufficiency of the Atonement He had made, my pardon sealed in His blood, and all the fulness and completeness of his justification. In a moment I believed and received the Gospel. Whatever my friend Madan[18] had said to me long before revived in all its clearness the demonstration of the spirit and with power. Unless the Almighty arms had been under me I think I should have died of gratitude and joy, and I could only look up to heaven in silent fear, overwhelmed with love and wonder.

Considering this amazing statement by William Cowper, one can understand why Louis Bredvold writes: "The poetry that grew out of these outwardly quiet years at Olney and Weston cannot be completely understood or read with sympathy without some knowledge of the evangelical religious movement of the day and its effect on Cowper."[19] This "evangelical religious movement" also had its emotional outbursts of a secular nature as when the "hidden love of

God," becomes with Shelley the "awful shadow of some unseen Power." And Charles Wesley's lines:

> I thirst, I faint, I die to prove
> The greatness of redeeming love,

can also be expressed by Shelley, as in the lines

> I die! I faint! I fail!

But when Shelley then writes:

> Let thy love in kisses rain
> On my lips and eyelids pale.

we are moving in an entirely dfferent direction. And the lyric poetry that was discovered in this new direction won for itself a deserved and honored place in the history of English literature. The spiritual lyric continued in its direction also, but for the eighteenth century at least, the culmination had been reached during this Pre-Romantic period by such intensity of expression as Charles Wesley's:

> Jesus, Lover of my soul,
> Let me to Thy bosom flee

and William Cowper's:

> Oh! for a closer walk with God,
> A calm and heavenly frame;
> A light to shine upon the road
> That leads me to the Lamb!

III. MYSTICS, MORAVIANS, AND METHODISTS

Throughout the eighteenth century there were German churches and German theologians in London. The German chapel at St. James, established in 1702 by Prince George, husband to Queen Anne, continued throughout the century as one of the most conspicuous churches in London "because of its being very exclusive."[1] It was attended by Germans attached to the Court as well as by distinguished visitors from Germany. The St. James chapel was under the general supervision of the Bishop of London, but always maintained a German chaplain and used a German translation of the *Book of Common Prayer*. The chapel at St. James became even more prominent after the ascension of George I. In a letter dated September, 1714, Anton Wilhelm Boehm, the Court Chaplain for Prince George and later for George I, mentions the expansion of his duties and the rapid growth of the German congregations at St. James, brought about by the coming of the Hannoverians.

> ... weil der König ein so groß Gefolge von Teutschen Bedienten um sich hat (etliche sagen bey die fünfhundert Personen) die der Engelschen Sprache nicht kündig sind, und dahero der Engländer Predigten nicht besuchen können.[2]

Older than the St. James German chapel was the St. Mary's German chapel in the Savoy, established in 1692, which was repaired and enlarged by George I in 1721. The popular German theologian Anthony Horneck was appointed preacher at the Savoy in 1671. In 1697 a German Reformed Church was established there, and by the middle of the eighteenth century there were four churches in the Savoy: the two German churches mentioned, a Quaker meeting house, and a French church. In 1743 a "Savoy Schule" was established there for the education of the German children living in London.

Other than the well known German chapels at St. James and at the Savoy, there was a chapel in Trinity Lane known as Trinity Lutheran

Church which had been German since 1618. The oldest German Lutheran church in London was probably the "Hamburg Church," so called because it was founded by German merchants from the Hansa city of Hamburg. Henry Jacobs also mentions other German churches: St. George's church in Goodmansfield, Zion's church in Brown's Lane, Spitalfields, and a German "Philadelphia Church" in Whitechapel. (143)

In 1698 a German church was established in Dublin, and during the eighteenth century there were also German churches in other large cities of England—Manchester, Liverpool, Hull, Bradford, and Bristol.

In 1738 John Wesley and Peter Böhler organized the "Fetter Lane Society" which was under strong German influence in both administration and membership. From this beginning the German Moravian congregations increased throughout the century, and as early as 1740 they had their own printing press at London where they published religious tracts, histories, and song books in both German and English.

It should be noted also that these German chapels were very important for the establishment and spread of German culture to America. Both the Lutherans and the Moravians had missions and colonies in America that were supplied and supported by the congregations in England. Heinrich Melchior Muhlenberg, the principal organizer of the German Lutheran congregations in Pennsylvania writes that the liturgy for these congregations was "after the model of that found in the order for the Savoy congregation in London." (Jacobs, 146) German presses were also established in America, one of the first being the press of Benjamin Franklin who published many things in German. Christoph Saur established a press in Philadelphia at which German books and tracts were published.

More important than the German churches, however, were the German theologians and scholars who attended these churches, and there are several names deserving mention here. Among the theologians who were active in the Savoy church was Anthony Horneck, who came to England about 1661. In 1664 he became chaplain of Queen's College, Oxford, and vicar of All Saints', Oxford. In 1668 he was elected a Fellow of the Royal Society and three years later was appointed preacher at the Savoy chapel in London. It was in this position that he gained his greatest fame as a social reformer and as a preacher. John Evelyn says Horneck's sermons were so popular that "chairs ... had to be placed outside the windows to accommodate his overflowing congregation."[3] According to Bishop Gilbert Burnet, Anthony Horneck and William Beveridge were instrumental in the establishment of "The Society for the Reformation of Manners" and similar societies. Clifford Towlson, speaking of the influence of Luther's writings on John and Charles Wesley, points out that much of Luther's influence in the eighteenth century came through the German Pietists in England and through these "religious societies, of which Horneck was the principal promoter."[4] The apogee of Horneck's career was reached with his appointment as "Chaplain to the King." He died in 1697 and is buried in Westminster Abbey. Indication that his influence was still prominent in the eighteenth century is in his writings, which were very popular and which were reprinted well into the century.[5]

Another German theologian who made his home in England was Johann Ernst Grabe, who came to England in 1697 on the advice of the "Father of Pietism" Philip Jakob Spener, in order to find a church "both Protestant and Episcopal." Having distinguished himself with his scholarship in Germany, he was welcomed and given a pension by William, which was continued by Queen Anne. He also received financial aid and support from his friend Robert Hartley. In England, Grabe's major accomplishment was the publication of the Alexandrine manuscript of the Septuagint, then in the Royal Library at St. James. The work was commissioned by Queen Anne, and Grabe received gifts and rewards from all over Europe for the publication. The work appeared in four volumes, only two of which were published during his lifetime, Volume I in 1707 and Volume IV in 1709. Grabe died in 1711 and the second and third volumes were published from his manuscript by Francis Lee and George Wigan. Grabe kept in contact with events in Germany through correspondence with German scholars, and he was especially close to the great scholar, writer, preacher, and translator, Gottfried Olearius. Olearius, who was also a close friend of the great classical scholar Johann Albert Fabricius, spent a year in England in 1693 studying Classical and Christian manuscripts. The lives and literary connections of Horneck, Grabe, Olearius, and Fabricius have not been fully examined, and I have mentioned them here primarily as a background for the discussion of the major religious movement in Germany of the late seventeenth and early eighteenth centuries, the *Collegium pietatis*.

Pietism, which became one of the moving forces in the changing nature of English culture in the eighteenth century, was the outgrowth of Philip Jakob Spener's Bible study group, the *Collegium pietatis*, organized by him in Frankfurt in 1670. The movement emphasized Bible reading, charity, Christian living, and especially, a personal relationship with God. Pietism never became a sect outside the Lutheran Church, but remained as Spener had intended it, "ecclesiola in ecclesia." His successor, August Hermann Francke, brought the movement to international notice with his famous "orphan house" at Halle University, which included among other things a publishing house and a hospital, and which provided for the complete physical, intellectual, and spiritual welfare of the students. The Halle system of supporting and educating orphans under August Hermann Francke was the beginning of the entire modern system of organized charities. John Wesley, who personally visited Halle, and Jonathan Edwards were strongly influenced by the charitable work done by the German Pietists, and both of these important religious leaders laid plans for orphanages of their own, based mainly on the pattern set at Halle. In fact, the "Holy Club" organized by Charles and John Wesley at Oxford was almost a duplicate of Spener's *Collegium pietatis*, and the fact that all the members of the "Holy Club" were familiar with the history of Pietism and the organization at Halle suggests that there was a succession of ideas from Francke to the Wesleys.[6] The intermediary between Halle and London who was most active in spreading the ideas and programs of the Pietists was Anthon Wilhelm Boehm.[7]

Boehm had become a student at Halle under Francke in 1693. At that time Halle had already become the center of Pietism and Boehm soon became closely associated with Spener's successor, August Hermann Francke. In 1701 Boehm came to London at the request of several German families who had been looking for a teacher from the Pietist school at Halle to supervise the education of their children. On his way to London he met Heinrich Wilhelm Ludolf, a learned orientalist and secretary to Prince George of Denmark, husband of Queen Anne. On Ludolf's recommendation Boehm became Prince George's chaplain at the German chapel in St. James in 1705, an office he retained under King George I and until his death in 1722. Prince George of Denmark surrounded himself with Halle Pietists including his Secretary, Ludolf, his Chaplain, Boehm, and his Chapel Musician, Johann Christian Jacobi, mentioned in Chapter II as one of the main contributors to the spread of Pietism in England through the translation and publication of German hymns.

Anton Wilhelm Boehm was largely responsible for the welfare of thousands of German emigrants who arrived in London in 1709.[8] The war of the Spanish Succession in 1707 had left many of the Germans of the Palatinate homeless and unemployed. In 1708 Joshua von Kocherthal led a small group of these people to England where, with the help of Boehm, he received the support of Queen Anne and was sent to New York where he and his associates established a settlement on the Hudson river which they called "Neuburg" (now Newburgh on the Hudson). The success of this emigration caused great excitement in the Palatinate and in 1709 the people from this area began a mass exodus to England with the hope of eventually reaching America. By October 1709 there were more than 13,000 Germans in London. Their chief intercessor at the court was Anton Wilhelm Boehm, as has been mentioned. They had another influential friend in London, however, a writer, who used his pen to solicit public support and financial aid for these homeless people. This friend was Daniel

Defoe. In nearly every edition of his *Review* from June 1709 until September of that year he discussed the plight of the Palatines and recommended legislation for their benefit. He encouraged generosity for their temporary relief and suggested means of employing and settling them permanently in England, rather than sending them to the colonies. In this effort he was assisted by Boehm who wrote an important tract in German to convince the Palatines that America was no land of milk and honey as they had been led to believe.[9] When a large group started for Ireland, Defoe recommended through his paper that they be given hospitable and kind treatment along the way. He recommended that those remaining (about 5,000) not be scattered and separated since that method of settling them "deprives them of all publick Exercise of Religious Worship, till they shall learn the English Tongue." (*Review*, Sept. 6, 1709) Defoe was probably acquainted with Anton Wilhelm Boehm since Boehm was exerting his influence at the court and Queen Anne provided relief funds for the refugees, while Defoe was exerting his influence on public opinion to assure the public that these German emigrants were worthy of this state relief. Defoe has given one of the most favorable accounts of these Germans in London.

> The People are sober, temperate, modest and courteous — There appears nothing loose, nothing immoral, nothing prophane among them — They are chearful under their misery, thankful in the Sense of their kind Reception here, perfectly subjected to what the Queen pleases to do for or with them, and behave themselves in all things without the least offence — They are now encamp'd in two camps at Black Heath and Camberwell, where they have entire liberty to go where they please all over the whole country — I have made dilligent Enquiry round them, and cannot find the least complaint of Wrong; the People live round them as secure, as if there were no such Folks there; not an Apple or Pear out of their Orchards, not a Hen or a Chicken lost, that I can possibly hear of.

> In matters of Business they appear laborious and skilful — Industrious to Labour, and ingenious in working and exceeding willing to be employ'd in any thing — In a word, they every way recommend themselves as a People, that shall bring a Blessing, and not a Curse to any Place that shall receive them. (*Review*, Aug. 6, 1709)

Defoe's acquaintance with these German emigrants possibly assisted him in forming a very close friendship with another German emigrant, a Mr. Kreutznaer, a "foreigner of Bremen," whose son Robinson Kreutznaer became internationally famous for his strange surprising adventures in the "new world."

Returning to the activities of Anton Wilhelm Boehm, we see that his first major literary undertaking was the translation and publication of Francke's history of the orphan house, *Pietas Hallensis*, to which he added a history of Pietism under Spener and Francke, and a catalogue of books that had been published at the Halle press. Boehm, following the example of his countryman of the previous decades, Anthony

Horneck, was also active in the organization and support of charitable societies in London. The second edition of his translation of Francke's *Nicodemus* (1709) was dedicated to "the Society for the Reformation of Manners," (one of the societies organized by Horneck) and in 1712 Boehm published: *The character of love . . . to which are added, the rules and orders for the management of a charitable society, set up at London in the year MDCCXII.* This and most of Boehm's writings were published by Joseph Downing who called himself "The German Bookseller."

In 1708 and again in 1710 Boehm published *The first principles of practical Christianity in questions and answers.* In 1710 and again in 1721 he published *Plain directions for reading the Holy Bible,* and in 1717, *Discourses and tracts for promoting the common interest of True Christianity.* In 1718 he published *The duty of Reformation,* and in 1720 *The doctrine of Godly Sorrow.* In all, Boehm wrote, edited, or translated more than forty different titles between 1705 and 1720, many of which went through numerous editions. His translations of Francke's history of the Halle orphan house, hospital, etc., were published through the century and into the nineteenth century. His translation of Francke's *Nicodemus* was abridged and published by John Wesley, and was in its sixth edition by 1786. All of these literary efforts, however, were peripheral to his most important work: the translation, publication, and dissemination of Johann Arndt's literary and theological masterpiece, *Vom wahren Christentum,* and most of Boehm's literary efforts, translations, sermons, histories of the Halle Pietism, and his *Plain directions for reading the Holy Bible* are but echoes of the ideas, metaphors, and analogies found in Arndt's work.

Vom wahren Christentum had become in Germany, along with the Bible, the major strength of the Protestant movement, and central to the particular phase of this movement known as Pietism. Spener could not praise it enough, Francke lived by it, and Boehm's major efforts in England were to prepare England for the reception of this work that had brought such a bounteous spiritual harvest in Germany. Excerpts from a few of Boehm's letters indicate his activity in this regard. In a letter of July 22, 1707 from London to "Christian Friends in Germany" Boehm tells of the success in getting books to the Germans in Pennsylvania and requests that they send him another shipment. In addition to the Bible and works of Tauler he wants "insonderheit auch Arndtii wahren Christenthum und zwar die kleinere Edition, um selbige unter desto mehrere auszubreiten." In another letter, London, May 19, 1710 to "Herrn P[astor] F[rancke] in H[alle] Boehm writes: "Die 44. Exemplaria von Arndii W[ahrem] C[hristenthum] wil ich, sobald sie ankommen, unter den Americanischen Christen aufs nützlichste auszustreuen suchen." In other letters he writes:

Ich habe dessen werthes Schreiben nebst dem Titul-Blat des in Holländischer Sprache edirten Arndtianischen Christenthums empfangen und mich über den Fleiss, den er in Ausgebung dieses Buches angewandt, erfreuet. Es hat ja Gott sein Siegel auf das Buch gedruckt. (Feb. 26, 1713)

Der Vorschlag, eine neue Engelsche Uebersetzung von Arndtii wahren Christentum zu machen, und in Schotland drucken zu lassen, hat mich sehr erfreuet, und danke Gott, der Ihnen solchen guten Vorsatz ins Hertze gegeben hat. (Jan. 27, 1715).

On another occasion (Aug. 3, 1713) Boehm tells about his efforts to get a French edition of *Vom wahren Christentum* published.

In addition to his efforts at importing German editions of Arndt's work, Boehm was very methodical in flooding England with both Latin and English translations. A brief history of this effort is somewhat as follows: *Vom wahren Christentum* was known in England as early as 1646 when Book I was translated and published, and Boehm found that this translation was still in circulation in the early eighteenth century. Shortly after his appointment as court chaplain in 1705, he began importing Latin editions of *De vero Christianismo* from Germany, and in 1708 he published a Latin edition in England. In 1709 he published *Short Instructions concerning the Principles of True Christianity*. This tract, which was a translation of certain passages of *Vom wahren Christentum*, was published by Boehm in order to give the public a sampling of the English translation he hoped to publish soon. The English translation appeared in two parts: Book I, translated in 1712 was by an anonymous friend of Boehm's, and Book II was translated by Boehm himself in 1714. Karl Schaible states that in addition to this edition "Boehm publicierte in London 1712 eine Übersetzung des vierten Theiles von Johann Arndt's Werk . . . in's Englische, mit dem Titel: "Book of Nature" und widmete es der Königin Anna."[10] I have not seen a reference to this separate printing of Book IV in any catalogue, but the specific title and the dedication to Queen Anne seems to indicate that Schaible was acquainted with such a printing.

Following the publication of the second part of *Vom wahren Christentum* in 1714, Boehm published *Discources and tracts for promoting the common interest of True Christianity* (1716), and *Several discources for promoting True Christianity* (1717). Both books were printed by "the German Bookseller" Joseph Downing. Boehm was not satisfied with the translation of Book I published in 1712 so he translated this Book himself and published a new edition of the entire four Books in 1720. The history of the publications of *Vom wahren Christentum* from this point on is somewhat obscure, but I have found reference to two further publications in the eighteenth century. William Law had in his library an English translation published in 1744, and John Wesley published parts of Boehm's translation in his *Christian Library* (1749-55).[11] Wesley had recognized the converting power of Arndt's masterpiece while on his trip to Germany in 1738. At Herrnhut he listened to the stories of a number of the Moravians, and not infrequently they attributed their conversion to Arndt's *Vom wahren Christentum*. In all, as far as I have been able to discover, there was in London: an English translation of Book I in 1646, a German Latin edition in 1707, an English Latin edition in 1708, excerpts of an English translation in 1709, an English translation of Book I in 1712, an English translation of Book IV titled "Book of Nature" in 1712, an English translation of Book II in 1714, an English translation of the entire work in 1720 and again in 1744, and excerpts of a translation in 1749.

A very interesting German edition appeared in 1751—not in England but in America. *Des hocherleuchteten theologie . . . sämtliche sechs geistreiche Bücher vom wahren Christenthum* (Philadelphia, Gedruckt und verlegt bey Benjamin Franklin und Johann Bohm). The Library of Congress Catalogue states that this edition of Arndt's *Vom wahren Christentum* by Benjamin Franklin was the largest book printed in Philadelphia to that time. There were, of course, many other English editions. One appeared in Boston in 1808 and another in Philadelphia in 1823. The edition I have before me was printed at Philadelphia in 1872, still based on the translation by Anton Wilhelm Boehm.

Vom wahren Christentum contains four "Books," and although Arndt wrote another two Books after the first four, they are considered something of an afterthought and are not usually published with the first four. The central theme of Book I is the fall of Adam and the consequent fallen state of mankind and its need for repentance. This serves as an introduction for Book II which discusses man's redemption from this fallen state and also the mission of Jesus Christ,

> as our help against the damnable and deadly poison of Original Sin, and the pernicious fruits thereof, as well as a protector against all the calamaties and evils both of the body and the soul.[12]

Book III brought Arndt the most criticism, just as Book IV brought him the most fame. The design of Book III according to Arndt is "to instruct [the reader] how to seek and find the kingdom of heaven within himself."

> And now, how glorious, how noble, and happy a thing is it, that our chief and most valuable treasure, that is, the kingdom of God, is not to be sought *without*, but to be found *within* us, that we continually carry it about with us, hidden from the world. (375)

This statement taken from Arndt's preface to Book III was heretical to a large body of learned theologians who decried the very suggestion of mysticism. Arndt did not help his cause with these critics when in Chapter I of Book III he cited Johannes Tauler as his guide.

> I shall first of all more generally in this chapter, and then more particularly, touch upon and explain the several heads of this doctrine, i.e. that the kingdom of God is to be found "in the inmost recesses of the soul" referring occasionally to the Theology of Dr. John Tauler, and quoting him as often as possible in his own words. And here I may remark, that as the Holy Scripture, great and sacred as it is regards the heart of man; so likewise, the whole divinity of Tauler aims at the inward man, the ground of the heart, and deepest recesses of the soul. (379)

Arndt cleverly defended himself from his critics by reminding them that it was their hero Martin Luther who had published the *Theologia Deutsch* (thought by Luther and Arndt to have been written by Tauler.)

Actually, Book III is about as reserved an exposition of the "inward life" as one could find and still call it "mystic." It is mystic in the way that the writings of Angelus Silesius or Daniel von Czepko are mystic, and there is nothing of the visionary or radical in Arndt's writings. The "true Christianity" could easily be called "practical Christianity" and this fact partially accounts for its great popularity among the German Pietists. There are "mystical" chapters in Book III such as, "of the great internal treasure of an enlightened believer," and, "the seat of God in the soul," but there are also chapters outlining the practical responsibilities that arise from this union with the Divine, such as, "God, the light of the soul, directing us not to judge our neighbors," and, "showing how our works may be rendered acceptable to God."

The last and literarily greatest of the *Four Books of True Christianity* Arndt says he copied from "the book of nature," (423) and vividly outlines the purpose of Book IV in the preface:

> The eminent prophet Moses exhibits to us two powerful witnesses of God, in the book of Creation. The first is the universe; the second is the inferior world, that is, Man .... We shall, therefore, introduce in the Book the testimony of both, that is, first, of the universe, and secondly, of the inferior world. Thus we shall learn that all creatures are, as it were, the guides and messengers of God, whereby we are to be brought to Christian knowledge, and also to God in Christ. (423)

Book IV is divided into two parts suggested in the preface: the relationships between the macrocosm and the microcosm. The first part consists of six chapters, each dealing with a day of the creation, the macrocosm, and the second part consists significantly of forty chapters "treating specially of man," the microcosm.

One aspect of the class of literature of which *Vom wahren Christentum* forms a part has been thoroughly discussed by Earl R. Wasserman in his article: "Nature Moralized: The Divine Analogy in the Eighteenth Century," *ELH* XXI, (1953).

> In *The Breaking of the Circle* Professor Marjorie Nicolson has dealt with the collapse of the divine analogy in the seventeenth century; my purpose here is to trace the residue of the idea throughout the eighteenth century and to evaluate the effect of the enervated form of the idea upon literary practice. (Wasserman, 42)

In spite of Marjorie Nicholson's thesis, as paraphrased here by Professor Wasserman, it should be mentioned that *in Germany* the concept of the divine analogy was strong throughout the seventeenth century and into the eighteenth. The work of Johann Arndt is an example of this analogy making and its popularity in Germany and is also an example of this same phenomenon in England. The entire fourth Book of *Vom wahren Christentum* is an extended analogy between nature, including man, and God. The analogies drawn between God and nature, however, never approach pantheism, and this, along with its constant practicality, is probably another reason for the perennial popularity of Arndt's work. As pointed out by Professor Wasserman, George Cheyne exercised great care in his analogy making to maintain an "infinite distance" between the Creator and His creation. "To deny the infinite distance would have been to risk hertical pantheism and to minimize faith; to deny the analogy would have been to deny the value of empiricism in arriving at divine truth." (43) Arndt in outlining the way to the "kindom within" is not so concerned with empiricism, but he is careful to make the distinction between the Creator and the creation, while at the same time retaining the analogy. Thus while discussing the sun Arndt says: "If God created so beautiful, refreshing, enlivening, clear, and shining a light; how much more lovely, comfortable, and refreshing a light must He be Himself?" (426) And he continues this thought by showing God's superiority to the creation.

> For whom did he create the sun? Certainly not for Himself, for He needeth not the sun, nor any other created light, being himself a light infinite and eternal. It was for our sakes, therefore, that He created it; so that every ray of light proceeding from the sun, is indeed a ray of divine love towards mankind. (426)

Having made this distinction, the analogy between the attributes of the sun (light) and God are extended.

> The light of the sun is pure and spotless; so is the love of God towards mankind. Hence also the divine wisdom, being a spotless light is, agreeably to this property of the sun, the spotless mirror of the divine majesty. As the light flows plentifully and freely from the sun; so the love of God descends plentifully upon us. As the sun shines freely upon all, without respect of persons; so the divine love overflows upon all mankind. As the light proceeds from the nature and essence of the sun; does the love of God flow from his very nature and essence. (426-7)

The analogy is extended even further by pointing out that "as the sun enlightens the world, so does Christ enlighten the soul." (427)

In Chapter II of Book IV, "of heaven, the work of the second day," Arndt makes the various analogies between the attributes of heaven and the attributes of God. Although many of his analogies seem fresh and original, many others, such as the circle being analogous to eternity, date Arndt quite well as a son of the Renaissance, and of classical antiquity.

54

> As to the stupendous height and compass of heaven, to which the earth is in comparison no more than a single point; how does it suggest to us the immense and unsearchable power and wisdom of God?... Does not its circular roundness remind us of the eternity of God? For of both there is neither beginning nor end. Does it not also tell us of his omnipresence? For as the heaven surrounds and compasses all things, so does the God of heaven support and comprehend all his creatures. (430)

The other four chapters of the first section of Book IV are of a similar nature. Arndt begins with a description of the work of the various periods of creation, makes the analogies, and usually completes the analogy with some kind of moral lesson. Chapter III contains a familiar pansophic analogy.

> Every herb and plant has its proper signature, which is nothing less than the inscription and handwriting of God, whereby he has most wonderfully and beautifully distinguished them all according to their virtues and qualities; and in many of them, the outward form is a token of their inward virtues. (433)

Chapter III is concerned with the period in creation when the waters were separated from the dry land, and the analogies are taken from these areas. Arndt discusses at some length the relationship between land and water and draws the analogies and morals.

> The mountains ought to remind us both of the protection of God and also of the Church of God ... Natural fountains, of which some are well known as possessing healing virtues, should remind us of the fountain of grace and salvation, the water of life, even Jesus Christ. (434-35)

Chapter IV is concerned with "the sun, moon, and stars, the work of the fourth day." Analogies are made on the nature of these heavenly bodies as well as on their functions, and in discussing the movement and function of the sun, stars, and moon, Arndt makes his strongest attempt to establish his analogies on a scientific basis, and he adds a light remonstrance to his less enlightened reader.

> As to the magnitude of the sun, moon, and stars, it is an error to imagine that they are really no larger than they appear to us.... Ocular demonstration convinces every man of this, that the more remote any object is, the less it appears. A nice disquisition of these matters the unlearned must leave to the astronomers, and be content religiously to admire what they do not understand. (445)

Arndt is speaking here to the "Stillen im Lande" and admonishing them to admire the creation of God although they do not understand its magnificent complexity. He follows this with an appropriate and comprehensible analogy.

> If we highly admire a well-built house with a fair prospect, furnished with good statues and pictures, and painted with great variety of colors, how much more ought we to look up with gratitude and astonishment to heaven, adorned with lights so many, and so stupendous. (445)

Chapter V is concerned with "the waters, and their productions, the work of the fifth day," and chapter six deals with "the living creatures, the work of the sixth day."

Part II of Book IV, "treating specially of man," the microcosm, discusses first the nature of God and then the nature of man, who is made in the image of God. The remainder of the book discusses the relationship between God and man, especially man's obligations to his Maker. Chapter XXI is concerned with "showing that from the service of man and the creatures, a union takes place between the visible world, man, and God." Again Arndt discusses the practical nature of Christianity by showing in Chapter XXIV that "man is obligated to love his neighbor as himself," and in Chapter XXVI that "charity is the foundation of the greatest strength." In the conclusion to Book IV of *Vom wahren Christentum* Arndt expresses the design and purpose of the whole:

> Hence too, Part II of this Fourth Book is not to be so understood, as if we could love God from our own carnal will; for love is a fruit of the Holy Spirit. This Part II. is, on the contrary only intended to show that, besides the Word of God, the Holy Scriptures, even our own heart and conscience may teach us, from the book of nature, and the light of nature, that we are bound to love God on account of his great love bestowed upon us, and manifested through the means of all his creatures. Such an argument, derived from nature, ought to convince every man, whether he be a heathen or a Christian, a believer or an unbeliever; and no one can refute it.

Arndt, with his insistence on the "kingdom within," his emphasis on the "heart and conscience," and "Holy Spirit" as guides in gleaning knowledge from the "book of nature" was, in an age of empiricism, enlightenment, and rationalism, an anachronism. But it must be remembered that he had died in 1621. As professor Wasserman points out, Dr. Cheyne, one of the strongest advocates of the "divine analogy" in the early eighteenth century was also an anachronism, "for the Platonism he called upon to reconcile the new empiricism with the old theology was too mystical for those temperate days." (Wasserman, 45) It is not entirely unlikely that Dr. Cheyne's mystical philosophy was flavored in part by Johann Arndt's true Christianity. At least it is certain that much of the philosophy of both Arndt and Cheyne had similar backgrounds and aims. Dr. Cheyne was certainly well steeped in the German mystical philosophy from Suso and Tauler to Jacob Boehme. It was from a book loaned to William Law by Dr. Cheyne that William Law first became acquainted with Jacob Boehme.

The "divine analogy" as a stimulus for artistic literary expression was, however, dying a slow death. In the words of Professor Wasserman:

> In the eighteenth century, then, there is to be found the last significant vestige of the myth of an analogically ordered universe, but greatly weakened by the

The union between man, nature, and God, if it was to be discovered, had to be discovered in the mind and not in the material world, and "the Romantics, taking their clue from the new psychology, but dissatisfied with mere associationism, now set out to find a more complex and closely integrated relationship of the shows of things and the desires of the mind." (Wasserman, 76)

The very distinction between the analogy-making of Arndt and that of the eighteenth century writers is that Arndt's analogy, although based on external observation of nature, is one that is to be taught by "our heart and conscience" and is not based on empirical truth. Being taught by "heart and conscience," combined with Arndt's emphasis on "the kingdom within," is much closer to what Professor Wasserman calls the "more complex and closely integrated relationship of the shows of things and the desires of the mind," than are the rationalistic analogies of the earlier eighteenth century. The fact that many of the Romantic poets in both Germany and England felt a strong attraction to the seventeenth century mystic thinkers seems to substantiate this view.

Although Arndt's emotional and mystical thought was, from one point of view, anachronistic in the early eighteenth-century empirical and rationalistic atmosphere, it was a thought that was soon to experience a triumphant restoration in a new form known as the "Great Awakening," and much of the subjective, emotional nature of the Romantic poets was a reflection of this religious atmosphere which was in large measure German-inspired. It was a religion stemming from the German Pietistic concepts of charity and good works combined with a belief in the mystical reception of the Spirit and a personal relationship with the Divine. Arndt had outlined the program and it had been put into practice at Halle and later at Herrnhut, and both the Pietists at Halle and the Moravians at Herrnhut found fertile ground in England for their missionary efforts. Jonathan Edwards, George Whitefield, John and Charles Wesley, John Cennick, John Gambold, William Law, and John Byrom were only some of the most prominent religious leaders and thinkers who were converts to the German Pietistic and mystic thought. The Wesleys, George Whitefield, John Gambold, and other members of the "Holy Club" had read Francke's *Pietas Hallensis* at Oxford in their student days, and the inspiration of these readings later gave rise to their orphan houses and hospitals. All these men were converts to the practical yet mystical Pietism of Francke and Anton Wilhelm Boehm, and they later became converts to the emotional and mystical Pietism of the Herrnhut Moravians, Spangenberg, Peter Böhler, and Count Zinzendorf. Arndt's *Vom wahren Christentum* is an embodiment, by anticipation, of both elements.

The empirical, rationalistic, and deistic tendencies in the religion of the early eighteenth century had perhaps strengthened the "reasonableness of Christianity" but they had at the same time greatly weakened its emotional spirit, and it was the bodily importation of German Pietism and mysticism that put this emotionalism back into religion in England. In a statement that seems more applicable to the early eighteenth century than to his own time, Johann Arndt writes:

> It is a notion too prevalent at this day, that men are very good Christians, if by reading or discourse they have attained to some kind of intellectual knowledge of Jesus Christ. This is that which generally passes under the name of Divinity, which the generality take to be nothing but a science, or a set of doctrines or opinions to be learned only in theory, not regarding the other most noble powers of the soul, namely, the will and the affections. But all these must be consecrated to God in Christ; and when thou hast done this, thou mayest assure thyself that thou are entirely dedicated to him. For there is a wide difference betwixt the understanding by which we know and the will or affections by which we love the Lord Jesus. (375)

Parallel with the importation of Arndt's *Vom wahren Christentum* was the importation of a more radical form of German mysticism, and William Law and John Byrom were the major importers. The importance of Law and Byrom as importers of German mysticism has been repeatedly discussed.[13] The catalogue of John Byrom's library and the catalogue of the library at King's Cliffe, which contains the library of William Law, both list dozens of important German works with which these two writers were familiar, in English translation, in Latin, and in the original German. William Law says he learned first of Jacob Boehme from *Fides et Ratio*, a book borrowed from Dr. Cheyne. Byrom learned of Boehme through Law, and so it continued. Both Byrom and Law learned German in order to read Jacob Boehme in the original, and were rewarded by discovering several other German writers of significance. Some of the important German authors whose works were in Byrom's library are: Anton Wilhelm Boehm, Johann Arndt, Johann Valentin Andreae, Jacob Boehme, August Hermann Francke, Anton Horneck, Quirinus Kuhlmann, Johannes Tauler, and Ludwig Zinzendorf. He also owned many German song books and the liturgy used in the German chapel at St. James: *Ein Gebeth-Büchlein aus der Englischen Liturgie . . . zum Gebrauch der Capelle P. Georgens von Danemarck*, (London, 1707). Some of the important German authors whose works were in Law's library are: Johann Arndt, Gottfried Arnold, Jacob Boehme, August Hermann Francke, Martin Luther, Johannes Scheffler, Johannes Tauler, and the *Theologia Germanica*, a 1632 German edition. His library also contained several German song books, grammars, dictionaries, and Bibles.[14]

As has often been pointed out, German mysticism, centered primarily in Jacob Boehme, had been popular in England for some time, but it was mainly through the efforts of William Law and John Byrom that this popularity was maintained in the eighteenth century. The finest English edition of Boehme, (1764-1781, 4 volumes), is still known as the "William Law Edition." The perpetuation of mysticism in England is perhaps best exemplified by the remark of Coleridge, who, in order to refute charges of plagiarism, stated that the similarity of his philosophy with that of the German philosopher Schelling was due to a common background of both in Jacob Boehme.

> Why need I be afraid? Say rather how dare I be ashamed of the Teutonic theosophist, Jacob Behmen? Many, indeed, and gross were his delusions; and such as furnish frequent and ample occasion for the triumph of the learned over the poor ignorant shoemaker who had dared think for himself. But while we remember that these delusions were such as might be anticipated from his utter want of all intellectual discipline and from his ignorance of rational psychology, let it not be forgotten that the latter defect he had in common with the most learned theologians of his age . . . .

> It would be but a mere act of justice to myself were I to warn my future readers that an identity of thought, or even similarity of phrase, will not be at all times a certain proof that the passage has been borrowed from Schelling, or that the conceptions were originally learnt from him. . . . Nor is this coincidence at all to be wondered at. We had studied in the same school; been disciplined by the same preparatory philosophy, namely, the writings of Kant; we had both equal obligations to the polar logic and dynamic philosophy of Giordano Bruno; and Schelling has lately and, as of recent acquisition, avowed that same affectionate reverence for the labours of Behmen and other mystics which I had formed at a much earlier period. The coincidence of Schelling's system with certain general ideas of Behmen he declares to have been mere coincidence; while my obligations have been more direct. He needs give to Behmen only feelings of sympathy; while I owe him a debt of gratitude.[15]

German mysticism had taken firm root in England before the time of William Law, but it was he who perpetuated and strengthened the movement so that it carried right through the Romantic period and gave rise to such astounding confessions of gratitude as the one quoted by Coleridge. Also, German Pietism had taken root in England before the time of John Wesley, but it was he who gave it a practical dynamism that carried it on through the eighteenth century and beyond, and earned for it the peculiar title: "Great Awakening." Bishop Warburton would place the credit for the religious revival on other shoulders when he says of Methodism in its infancy: "William Law was the father, and Count Zinzendorf rocked the cradle." Warburton has reference here to the influence of William Law's *Serious Call* and the influence of the Moravians led by Count Zinzendorf. These are, of course, genuine and important influences in the life of John Wesley, but one cannot so easily overlook his dynamic and energetic leadership, without which Methodism would never have left the Moravian "Fetter Lane Society."

The Methodist relations with the Moravians has been discussed in the chapter on the German hymn. As a conclusion to the discussion of German theologians in England, however, a note on Nicholas Ludwig, Count von Zinzendorf is appropriate here.

Zinzendorf was in England many times from 1737 on, and he was especially active in England between the years 1751 and 1754 when the English Moravian Church was at the peak of its popularity. Actually there were German Moravians in England in increasing numbers from as early as 1735, but it was always the powerful personality of Count Zinzendorf that provided the motivating force to the movement. This personality, however, was as repulsive to some as attractive to others, and although John Wesley referred to Herrnhut with devoted sincerity as "the place where the Christians live," and Charles Wesley when with the Moravians thought himself "in a quire [sic] of Angels," the external pompousness of Count Zinzendorf did not correspond with their concepts of piety and humility. Zinzendorf was probably as pious and humble as either of the Wesleys although it was a different type of humility, and he was certainly as sincere and dedicated.

> Zinzendorfs Grösse liegt in seinem von Liebe zum Heillande brennenden Herzen; "ich habe nur eine Passion; die ist Er, nur Er." In diesem Beruf ging all sein Denken und Sinnen auf; sein ganzes Leben, Geist, Herz, Hab und Gut hat er ihm gewidmet und alle Vortheile, welche Geburt, Stand und Bildung ihm darboten wusste er dieser seiner Lebensaufgabe dienstbar zu machen.[16]

This paragraph epitomizes the personality of Zinzendorf. He was completely dedicated to his labors for his Savior; "ich habe nur eine Passion; die ist Er, nur Er." At the same time however, he was a Count, well educated, the master of great tracts of land, and he knew how to use these advantages to the furthering of his purposes. Wesley could not conceive of a rich, noble, and extremely popular Count (popular almost to the point of adoration) as a devoted follower of Christ. In a letter to the Brethren published by Wesley in 1740, after he had severed relations with the Moravian organization, he could still praise them for their sincerity. "I cannot but rejoice in your steadfast faith, in your love to our blessed Redeemer, your deadness to the world; your meekness, temperance, chastity, and love of one another." However, Wesley could not refrain from pointing out one of their greatest weaknesses. "Is not the Count all in all? Are not the rest mere shadows; calling him Rabbi; almost implicitly both believing and obeying him?" (quoted from Towlson, 74)

The break between the Methodist and the Moravian has been fully treated by Clifford Towlson. It is sufficient here to point out the fact that the major reason for this break was a personality clash between the two leaders, and not the doctrinal differences often mentioned.

60

One of the doctrinal differences was the claim of apostolic succession by the Moravians who wanted to trace their history back to Jan Hus. Since the Methodists were considered by many to be a new religion, in spite of John Wesley's repeated declarations to the contrary, the Moravians were careful to point out the difference.

> Whosoever reckons that those persons in England who are usually called Moravians and those who are called Methodists are the same, he is mistaken. That they are not the same is manifest enough out of the declaration of Louis, late Bishop and Trustee of the Brethren's Church.

This advertisement in the *London Daily Post* was answered by John Wesley who was not as concerned with the declaration as with the author of the declaration.

> The Methodists, so-called, heartily thank brother Louis for his Declaration; as they count it no honour to be in any connexion either with him or his Brethren. But why is he ashamed of his name? The Count's name is Ludwig, not Louis; no more than mine is Jean or Giovanni.... Was there ever such a Proteus under the sun as this Lord Freydeck, Domine de Thurstain, etc., etc.? For he has almost as many names as he has faces or shapes. Oh when will he learn (with all his learning) "simplicity and Godly sincerity"? (Towlson, 131)

The qualities of personality that offended John Wesley did not offend everyone, however. Zinzendorf was adored by his humble followers and he was esteemed by the upper classes of society. He gave lectures at Oxford and was a personal friend of the Bishops of London, Lincoln, and Worcester. He was given a 99 year lease on Lindsey House in Chelsea by Sir Hans Sloane, President of the Royal Society. He was an attraction wherever he went, and it cannot be denied that he earlier captivated the hearts of both John and Charles Wesley. The fact that they had been at first so completely enraptured by him may account for a great deal of their later animosity.

The personal attraction and popularity of Zinzendorf was an important factor in bringing Germany and things German to the knowledge of the English public, and it was during and just following this period that much German sentimental and religious literature became more popular in England. As a more direct stimulation to literature Zinzendorf is important as the author of over 2,000 hymns, and many of these were translated into English. There was a time, however, spoken of as "the sifting period," when Zinzendorf's popularity waned somewhat with certain segments of society. The doctrines and practices of the Moravians became in their extreme form, repugnant to those who were more conventional in their religious attitudes. Zinzendorf's poetry, which reflects these doctrines, came to speak with increasing familiarity of Jesus as the "bridegroom of the soul," which, although no new concept, was offensive to many. It must be admitted, however, that the imagery used by Zinzendorf to illustrate this "union of the soul with her Heavenly Bridegroom" did not reach the extremes of the imagery used by many Baroque poets in Germany, such as Johann Rist's:

> Ich lig und seuffze mit Begier,
> O allerschönste Braut, nach dir . . .

More repulsive, however, was the imagery placing extreme emphasis on the wounds of Christ. This poetry soon became known as the "blood and wounds hymns." John Wesley held these hymns up to ridicule in his *Hymns extracted from the Brethren's Book* (1749). In 1751 Gerhardt Tersteegen, another great German poet, wrote Zinzendorf a "Warnungsschreiben" pointing out the exaggerated piety of the Moravian practices and warning them of "Leichtsinnigkeit." Zinzendorf was evidently grateful for Tersteegen's criticism, and in 1754 he carefully omitted any hymns that might have been offensive from the "London" song book.

CONCLUSION

Only the more prominent German theologians and religious leaders have been mentioned in this survey. But even from this survey it is obvious that the pattern of thought coming from Germany during the first half of the eighteenth century did not fit the Enlightenment pattern of thought so popular in England at the time. German thought was moving in an entirely different direction from the "Christianity not mysterious," "chain of being" pattern.

One of the salient features of German Romanticism, and this feature is reflected somewhat in English Romanticism, is that it remains one of the very few moments in the history of human culture when the outstanding intellectuals were able to form a synthesis of thought which unified the epistemological polarity with which mankind is normally plagued. These thinkers saw a perfection of humanity in the union of the empirical-rational quest for truth with the intuitive-mystic quest for truth. For Schiller this was the "Totalität des Lebens" personified in the "schöne Seele," and for Friedrich Schlegel this was the "Universalität," and the "Paradoxie des Lebens." The truth seeker should be both reflective and intuitive, "sentimental" and "naiv." The English thinker who most prominently reflected these ideas was Samuel Taylor Coleridge, who wanted to "keep alive the heart in the head," and who felt "that all the products of the *mere* reflective faculty partook of death, and were as the rattling twigs and sprays in winter." The background to this phenomenon can be traced immediately to the mysticism and Pietism of the seventeenth and eighteenth centuries; to the irrationality that constantly threatened to destroy the cherished hopes of the Enlightenment philosophers who thought the happiness of the human race could be achieved by the simple application of "reason." This irrationality provided a counter to the onesidedness of the Enlightenment. The Pietists railed against the "pride" of the educated, the educated railed against the "pride" of man in general, but particularly the sophisticated, and the sophisticated railed against the "enthusiasm" of the Pietists and mystics. Perhaps the irony of this raillery is that both poles of thought produced thinkers of such genius that the Romanticists at the end of the century were somewhat compelled into a synthesis. The surface reaction during the dispute, however, was kinder to the empirical-rational thinkers than to the intuitive-mystic "enthusiasts." Perhaps that is why Coleridge felt inclined to speak in defense of that group we would now label "anti-intellectual." Regardless of the labels, the importance of German thought in changing the direction of the Enlightenment in England has only been suggested in this survey, but it cannot continue to be neglected by scholars treating the literary history of this period if we are to come to a clearer understanding of the German-English relations in the eighteenth century. How could one, for example, refuse to take seriously the following statement by Coleridge and still hope to present a proper interpretation of the literature of his period—and since?

> One assertion I will venture to make, as suggested by my own experience, that there exist folios on the human understanding and the nature of man which would have a far juster claim to their high rank and celebrity, if in the whole huge volume there could be found as much fulness of *heart and intellect* [italics mine] as burst forth in many a simple page of George Fox, Jacob Behmen, and even of Behmen's commentator, the pious and fervid William Law.

> The feeling of gratitude which I cherish towards these men has caused me to digress further than I had foreseen or proposed; but to have passed them over in an historical sketch of my literary life and opinions would have seemed to me like the denial of a debt, the concealment of a boon. For the writings of these mystics acted in no slight degree to prevent my mind from being imprisoned within the outline of any single dogmatic system. They contributed to keep alive the heart in the head; gave me an indistinct, yet stirring and working presentment, that all the products of the mere reflective faculty partook of death, and were as the rattling twigs and sprays in winter into which a sap was yet to be propelled from some root to which I had not penetrated, if they were to afford my soul either food or shelter. If they were too often a moving cloud of smoke to me by day, yet they were always a pillar of fire throughout the night, during my wanderings through the wilderness of doubt, and enabled me to skirt, without crossing, the sandy deserts of utter unbelief.[17]

IV. GERMANS RESIDENT IN ENGLAND: MUSICIANS, ARTISTS, AND GERMANS IN THE ROYAL SOCIETY

"For half a century English music was Handel and the opera,"[1] writes George Sherburn, and, for a one sentence statement on the state of music in England in the early eighteenth century, this is fairly accurate. Of course, Handel had much competition from Italian composers and from the ballad opera, but in both quality and quantity of musical composition, he had no equal. There were other German musicians in England at the time, however, and although they were overshadowed by the genius of Handel they do deserve recognition for the part they played in the development of English culture through this part of the century, and especially because of their interrelations to the literature of the day.

One reason for the abundance of German musicians in England at this time, as in the case of Handel, was the Hannoverian Court; but there were Germans who had gained a name in London music circles before the coming of the Hannoverians. About 1685 a German composer by the name of Gottfried Finger arrived in London and began composing sonatas for strings in collaboration with another German musician and music teacher, Gottfried Keller. (An amusing confusion in *Grove's Dictionary of Music and Musicians* makes this now obscure German musician the author of *Die Leute von Seldwyla*.) In 1695 Finger turned his talents to the English stage and began composing "instrumental act tunes" for the current plays. For the next ten years he provided music for the London stage. Some of the most popular plays for which he composed music were: Congreve's *Love for Love*, and *The Mourning Bride*; Lansdowne's *She-Gallants*; Dryden's *The Husband his own Cuckold*; Joseph Harris' *The City Bride*; Dilke's *The City Lady*; Mrs. Trotter's *Love at a Loss*; Colley Cibber's *Love makes a Man*; and George Farquhar's *Sir Harry Wildair*. Finger had also collaborated with John Eccles in writing the music for Motteaux's masque *The Loves of Mars and Venus*, and with Daniel Purcell in writing the music for Lee's *The Rival Queens*. In 1701 he entered a contest to set the music for Congreve's *The Judgment of Paris*. Biographers say that his disgust at winning only fourth prize caused him to leave London, but he was still in London as late as 1706. He did eventually return to Germany, however, and perhaps felt more appreciated there. He gained a reputation in Germany as a composer of operas and apparently did not return to London.

Johann Christopher Pepusch, having gained a reputation in Germany as a brilliant harpist at the age of fourteen, came to London in 1688 and gained greater fame as a teacher of the science of harmony. He had many notable musicians among his pupils and he was assisted in some of his studies on harmonics by the mathematician De Moivre. In 1696 the Drury Lane Theater was rebuilt, having burned in 1672, and was opened under the direction of Colley Cibber. Pepusch became a player there and then began to write for the opera company. In 1710 he took an active part in the establishment of the "Accademy of Ancient Music," and in 1713 he was granted a Doctor of Music degree from Oxford. In 1724 he made plans with George Berkeley for the establishment of a college in Bermuda and both Berkeley and Pepusch set out for Bermuda with this project in mind, but the ship was wrecked and they both returned to England. Although Berkeley did later go to America, Pepusch remained in England and followed his musical career.

In 1737 Pepusch became organist in the Charterhouse in London and retained this position until his death in 1752. In 1745 he was named a Fellow of the Royal Society for his work on harmonics, but his real fame was gained as a musician and as a director of the theater at Lincoln's Inn Fields known as the "little Haymarket."

The Lincoln's Inn Fields theater had been errected in 1714 by Christopher Rich and opened by his son John Rich. John Rich began to produce a number of pantomimes and masques with Pepusch as director and with Pepusch and another German, John Galliard, as principal musicians. In addition to his work as director and musician, he found time to write the music for a number of the masques and pantomimes Rich produced, including Colley Cibber's *Myrtillo* (1715), *Venus and Adonis* (1715), *Appollo and Daphne* (1716), *Death of Dido* (1716), *Perseus and Andromeda* (1717), and *Diocletian* (1724), He is still primarily remembered, however, (when he is remembered at all) as the composer of the music for John Gay's *Beggar's Opera*. Colley Cibber had refused to produce the *Beggar's Opera* at the Drury Lane Theater, but John Rich had had such success with pantomimes and masques that he ventured to produce it, and the oft repeated story is that this venture "made Rich gay and made Gay rich." There seems to be no record of what it made Pepusch but one must assume that as a musician it made him gayer than rich. Follwing his success with the *Beggar's Opera*, Pepusch wrote the music for *Polly*, John Gay's sequel to the *Beggar's Opera*.

Pepusch's countryman and fellow composer at the Lincoln's Inn Fields theater was Johann Ernst Galliard. Galliard had been the chamber musician for Prince George of Denmark, and when Anne became queen in 1702 Galliard accompanied George to England, and subsequently became the chamber musician to Catherine, the widow of Charles II. In 1712 he wrote the music for John Hughes' *Calypso and Telemachus*. He also wrote several cantatas to the texts of Matthew Prior, Congreve, and Hughes. After John Rich opened the Lincoln's Inn Fields theater Galliard began composing for him, and in this connection he wrote the music for *Pan and Syrinx* (1717), *Jupiter and Europa* (1723), *The Necromancer, or Harlequin Faustus* (1723), *The Loves of Pluto and Prosperpine* (1725), *Apollo and Daphne* (1726), *The Royal Chase, or, Merlin's Cave* (1736), as well as many other pantomimes, cantatas, songs, and solos for many instruments.

The life of the greatest of German musicians in the early eighteenth century, Georg Friedrich Handel, is too well known to need retelling in any detail here. He was raised and educated at Halle and came to London first in 1710 at the age of 25, having already gained a reputation for his operas composed in Germany and Italy. He was encouraged by the court and nobility to compose an opera in London and in 1710 he composed *Rinaldo*, which was produced by Aaron Hill at the Haymarket theater, known then as the Queen's theater. He soon returned to Germany, however, and became the chapel musician at the court in Hannover. A second visit to England in 1712 turned out to be a permanent one. When his patron at Hannover became George I, King of England, in 1714, there were apparently some strained relations between the two Georges, the main reason being that Handel had refused to return to Hannover in 1712. These relations soon improved, however, and the 200 pound pension given Handel by Queen Anne was increased to 600 by George I and was continued by George II. Handel lived with the Earl of Burlington and soon became one of the leading members of London society. In 1716 he accompanied the King to Hannover and also visited Halle and Hamburg. At this time he composed the music for an oratorio written by the great German poet Barthold Heinrich Brockes, "Der für die Sünden der Welt gemarterte und sterbende Jesus." The oratorio was very popular in Germany and was performed in London as soon as Handel returned in 1716. It has generally been assumed that no one in England had ever heard of Brockes before he published his *Irdisches Vergnügen in Gott* beginning in 1721, although his name was associated with Handel's as early as 1716.

It was this oratorio by Brockes and Handel that began Brockes' reputation in England, although knowledge of him as the author of the *Irdisches Vergnügen in Gott* cetainly increased his fame. By 1731 the author of the *Republic of Letters* could refer to Brockes as: "One of those sublime Geniuses."[2]

In 1719 Handel and J. J. Heidegger, a Swiss composer and manager of the Haymarket theater, formed the Royal Academy of Music. Heidegger, who had come to England early in the eighteenth century managed the Haymarket theater from 1713 until 1741, with only a few years interruption. Under his management Handel became director of the opera company there and their Royal Academy of Music enjoyed great success until 1728 when the ballad opera at the Lincoln's Inn Fields theater began to rise in popularity. The Royal Academy was terminated, but Handel and Heidegger formed a new company and continued to produce Handel's operas. In 1732 John Rich who had been so successful with the ballad opera moved into the new Covent Garden theater, and Frederick, the Prince of Wales, established an opera company at Lincoln's Inn Fields called "the opera of nobility" in an attempt to rival Handel and at the same time to embarrass Handel's patron, the King. With the audience now divided three ways, Handel and Heidegger began losing money, and in 1734 they terminated their second opera company. The "opera of nobility" was quite successful, mainly because of political reasons, and leased the King's theater just vacated by Handel. In an interesting switch, Handel took over the vacated Lincoln's Inn Fields theater and continued to produce his operas of high quality which were unfortunately out of popularity. In 1735 he moved to the Covent Garden and wrote for John Rich. In 1737 the opera company under the sponsorship of the Prince of Wales in the Haymarket had to disband, mainly because of bad management, and Heidegger was asked to take over the management of the Haymarket theater again. Handel then began to turn more and more toward the music for which he is still most famous, the oratorio. Between 1740 and his death in 1759 he wrote more than a dozen full scale oratorios. The most famous of these, *The Messiah*, was first performed in Dublin in 1742.

His friend Heidegger continued to manage the Haymarket theater with the patronage of George II, and at the same time wrote many librettos of his own. Heidegger, like Handel, was very well known in London society and was a friend of Fielding, Pope, and many other famous writers. John Hughes dedicated one of his major works to him: *Charon: or the Ferry Boat, A Vision*. Heidegger was mentioned occasionally in the *Spectator* and received a somewhat infamous place in Pope's *Dunciad*. It seems that Heidegger was notorious for his ugliness. In the first book of the *Dunciad* Pope wrote:

And lo, her bird (a monster of a fowl)
Something betwixt a Heideggre and owl.

Handel, who was greatly esteemed by Pope, fared much better in the *Dunciad*. Lamenting the dullness of the Italian opera Pope wrote:

> But soon, ah! soon, rebellion will commence,
> If music meanly borrows aid from sense:
> Strong in new arms, lo! giant Handel stands,
> Like bold Briareus with his hundred hands;
> To stir, to rouse, to shake the soul he comes,
> And Jove's own thunders follow Mars' drums. (IV, 63ff.)

Pope was not prejudiced against German music as were many of his contemporaries, at least he ventured to obtain an opinion from his friend Dr. Arbuthnot who replied: "Conceive the highest that you can of his abilities and they are much beyond anything that you can conceive."[3] In seeking an opinion of one who understood music he showed more wisdom than Dr. Johnson who visited one of Handel's operas to form his own opinion and remarked to David Garrick: "I say, Davy, music is nothing but a noise that is less disagreeable than some others."[4] This is hardly a valid judgment from one who applauded the orchestra as it was tuning and then remarked when informed of his error: "And I heard nothing finer the whole evening."[5] Pope, Arbuthnot, and Handel collaborated on occasions. Pope and Arbuthnot wrote the libretto for the oratorio *Esther* and Handel wrote the music. The same arrangement was made for the secular choral works *Acis and Galatea* and *Semele*.

From these historical facts it is obvious that there was a close relationship between the German musicians in England and the important writers and critics, and that this relationship exerted an influence on the literature and general culture. Not only were there several musical-literary collaborations, but there were also music theorists and critics who contributed significantly to the development of English literature. Harold Jantz, in his important article "German Baroque Literature," has suggested the importance of opera criticism for the development of the drama. The entire concept of drama as an imitation of nature broke down when critics tried to appraise the opera as drama. Addison could ridicule the "unnaturalness" of the opera when the hero sings an aria while he is dying, but the fact that this same opera was great art in spite of its "unnaturalness" was a continual disturbance to the critics. How could the literary critics continue to praise Handel as a great artist, a "sublime genius," and with consistency speak disparagingly of his dramatic operas for their failure to imitate nature? Handel was as much of an unmanagable genius as was Shakespeare for the critics. Both produced sublime art, but neither conformed to the prescribed pattern. Shakespeare had an excuse. He produced his art before the prescribed pattern for drama had been made into law. Handel, however, was simply being obstinate. Minor critics throughout the early part of the century saw the futility and foolishness of the attempt to fit art into a mold. There is no dramatic illusion on the stage, and drama is not an imitation of nature. Johann Elias Schlegel (1719-1749) a dramatic poet and theorist, the uncle of Friedrich and Wilhelm, pointed out that the stage is never in this room or that house, but it is always in the theater.

> . . . wenn die Personen nur deswegen in den angezeigten Saal oder Garten kommen, um auf die Schaubühne zu treten: so würde der Verfasser des Schauspiels am besten getan haben, an Statt der Worte: Der Schauplatz ist ein Saal in Elimenens Hause, unter das Verzeichniss seiner Personen zu setzen: Der Schauplatz ist auf dem Theater.[6]

It remained for the greater critics, Lessing and Samuel Johnson, however, to see and express this idea clearly. Johnson in his important *Preface* (1765) to his edition of Shakespeare makes this penetrating remark:

> The objection arising from the impossibility of passing the first hour at Alexandria, and the next at Rome, supposes, that when the play opens, the spectator really imagines himself at Alexandria, and believes that his walk to the theatre has been a voyage to Egypt, and that he lives in the days of Antony and Cleopatra. Surely he that imagines this may imagine more.[7]

And he that imagines this may imagine that an opera is not attempting to imitate nature, and that when the hero dies while singing an aria he is really expressing something that cannot be imitated. The role of music and the history of the criticism of the opera and the relationship of this criticism to the drama and the changing critical attitudes in the eighteenth century has never been fully investigated.[8]

To return to the history of German musicians in England, there are a few other names that must be mentioned. An important but now forgotten composer who lived in England was Johann Friedrich Lampe who came to England from Saxony in 1725. As an author he was known for *A Plain and Compendious Method of Teaching Thorough Bass* (1737), and *Art of Musick* (1740). His major contribution to English culture, however, was his composition of operas and ballad operas. Between 1730 and 1745 he had sixteen major compositions produced on the London stage. So, we see that Handel was not the only German opera composer of some popularity. Lampe was engaged by John Rich to compose for the Covent Garden Theater but he also composed for J. J. Heidegger at the Haymarket. In 1732 he wrote the music for Henry Carey's *Amelia* and for Thomas Lediard's *Britannia*. Thomas Lediard was the secretary to the English ambassador at Hamburg, Sir Cyril Wich, and his contribution to German culture in England is discussed further in Chapter V. In 1733 Lampe wrote the music for Fielding's *The Opera of Operas, or Tom Thumb the Great*, which was produced at the Drury Lane theater by Colley Cibber. In this same year Heidegger produced a mock opera by Henry Carey and Johann Lampe called *Chrononhotonthologos*! This was a burlesque of the extravagance of love and heroism in the Italian opera that was so popular at the time, and its success encouraged Carey and Lampe to produce *The Dragon of Wantley* in 1737. *The Dragon of Wantley* had the distinction of being the only ballad opera to enjoy a longer run than Gay's *Beggar's Opera*, and it is said to have been Handel's favorite among the comic operas, perhaps because it was another satire on the Italians who were his major competitors. In 1738 Carey and Lampe wrote another comic opera called *Margery, or, a worse Plague than the Dragon*. Shortly after this, Lampe became a convert and close friend of Charles Wesley, and in 1746 he wrote the music for Wesley's *Hymns on the Great Festivals and other Occasions*, which made this collection one of Wesley's most popular. In 1746 Lampe also wrote a "Kirchen-Musik" to celebrate the repression of the Stuart rebellion of 1745, and this piece was sung in German at the Savoy chapel and then published in Hannover. In 1748 and 1749 Lampe lived in Dublin and in 1750 he went to Edinburgh where he died in 1751.

Karl Friedrich Weidemann, a German flutist and composer, came to England about 1726 and 1738 became conductor of the "King's Band of Musick." It seems that the Germans in England were famous for starting societies, and *Grove's Dictionary* says "it was Weidemann who, with Festing first conceived the idea of a musical benevolent society, which ultimately took form as the Royal Society of Musicians."

Two other important musicians came to England from Germany who added considerably to English musical culture at this time: Karl Friedrich Abel and Johann Christian Bach. Abel arrived in London in 1759 and his friend Bach arrived in 1762. Abel was a popular virtuoso on the Viola da gamba and on the harp, and he became quite famous as an improvisor and composer while serving as chamber musician to the queen. This position he received through the Duke of York on whose recommendations he had first come to London.

Johann Christian Bach, sometimes referred to as the "London Bach," was the eleventh and youngest son of Johann Sebastian Bach. He was a good organist and harpist, and also a chamber musician to the queen. In our own time his reputation has been revived and he is being spoken of as one of the great German composers. He gave many concerts with Karl Abel, and it was Christian Bach who befriended the Mozart family when they came to London and arranged for their introduction at the court and for the concerts by the young Mozart.

Two other German composers who spent some time in England

were Johann Adolf Hasse and Christoph von Gluck. Hasse had studied first in Hamburg where he was a friend of the poet Johann Ulrich König, and where he sang in the opera house under the direction of Reinhold Keiser. In 1723 he went to Italy for further training and while there married the most famous prima donna of the day, Faustina Bordoni. In 1733 he spent some time in London where he wrote and produced his opera *Artaxerxes*. He was in London again in 1740 when he was asked to manage an opera company in rivalry with his countryman Handel but he rejected the offer and soon left London.

Christoph von Gluck came to England in 1745 to write for the King's theater then under the direction of Lord Middlesex. In 1746 he composed in London *Der Sturz der Giganten oder La Caduta dei Giganti*, and dedicated it to Lord Cumberland for his victory over the pretender. In the same year he wrote *Piramo e Tisbe*, and *Artamene*, but although he was hailed as another Handel he was dissatisfied with his success and soon left England.

B. GERMAN ARTISTS

The most well-known German Painter in England in the early 18th century was Sir Godfrey Kneller who arrived in London in 1675 with recommendations from Jacob del Böe, a Hamburg art collector. Kneller had studied in Amsterdam with Ferdinand Bol in 1668 and had then gone to Italy with his brother Johann Zacharias who was also a painter. In England Godfrey Kneller stayed with a Hamburg merchant named Jonathan Banks, and through him made the acquaintance of James Vernon, the secretary to the Duke of Monmouth, whose portrait he painted in 1678. Soon after, he painted the portrait of Charles II and immediately gained a reputation as one of the best painters in the country. In 1684 Charles sent him to France to paint the portrait of Louis XIV at Louis' request. In 1692 Kneller was knighted, in 1695 was given an annual pension of 200 pounds, and in 1711 he became the director of the newly founded Academy of Painting. Kneller remained court painter and under George I in 1715 he was made a Baronet. During this time, Kneller painted over 300 portraits including portraits of ten reigning monarchs and forty-eight portraits of members of the "Kit-Cat-Club," as well as many other prominent persons in England. Among those whose portraits he painted were: John Locke, Isaac Newton, William Congreve, John Dryden, John Gay, Alexander Pope, Isaac Watts, Samuel Pepys, Sir Hans Sloane, John Addison, Prince George of Denmark, and Thomas Sprat. Special mention must be made of one other portrait. Kneller's portrait of Matthew Prior is certainly a masterpiece and one of the most marvellous examples of portrait painting in the long history of art.[9]

In addition to contributing greatly to the artistic culture of England through his painting, Kneller contributed to the development of cultural relations between England and Germany, and he encouraged his friend Heinrich Offelen to publish a German-English and English-German dictionary and grammar. This Offelen did in 1687 and dedicated the book to Prince George: *Zweyfache Gründlich Sprach-Lehr für Hoch-teutsch english, und für Engländer hochteutsch zu lernen, durch Henricum Offelen, Juris utriusque Doctor, Professor der: französischen, spanischen, italienischen, lateinischen, englischen, hochteutschen und niederteutschen Sprachen.*

A well known painter who came to England in 1721 was Baltasar Denner. Denner had gained a reputation in Hamburg and in 1713 he was called to the court in Copenhagen to work there. In 1720 he was in Wolfenbüttel, and while there and in Hannover he met many of the nobility from England. Denner was a good friend of the Hamburg poets Barthold Heinrich Brockes, Friedrich von Hagedorn, and Christian Weichmann, and both Hagedorn and Weichmann spent considerable time in England themselves. Denner went to England in 1721 and stayed until 1728 when he returned to Hamburg.

Georg Dionys Ehret was a botanical painter who came to England about 1735 and then studied in Paris and later in Holland with Linnaeus before coming to England for the second time about 1740. He found a patron in Sir Hans Sloane who was at that time President of the Royal Society. While in Holland Ehret had illustrated Linnaeus' *Hortus Cliffortianus*, and after his arrival in England Sir Hans Sloane commissioned him to draw the illustrations for the *Transactions of the Royal Society*. He became a member of both the Royal Academy and the Royal Society. Patrick Browne named the genus *Ehretia* in his honor and this designation was adopted by Linnaeus. Ehret worket in London until his death in 1770.

Johann Gottfried Haid formed an interesting connection between London art circles and the Vienna Academy. Haid gained a reputation and a patron in Vienna with his painting of the Royal Family of Maria Theresia, and he came to England with the support of the Viennese court in 1760. In England he worked and studied with John Boydell and returned to Vienna in 1766.

Another well known painter who lived in England was Johann Zoffany, who came to England in 1758, but nearly starved to death before he was employed by Stephen Rimbault, a clock-maker. He then began working for Benjamin Wilson as a drapery painter. There are various stories about his rise to prominence in the art circles. One story is that Lord Bute was attracted to a picture done by Zoffany of Garrick in the character of Hamlet, depicting what Dr. Johnson called "the start that started the Ghost." Zoffany was introduced at court and in 1769 became a member of the Royal Academy. His greatest fame came from his paintings of actors in character. He travelled widely but maintained a residence in England where he died in 1810.

Perhaps the most important artist to come to England from Germany in the eighteenth century was Heinrich Füssli, who gained fame as a writer and translator as well as a painter and President of the Royal Academy. It is also now becoming clear that Füssli is probably more responsible than any other single person for the new wave of Hellenism that became evident in English art and literature in the late eighteenth century. The man most responsible for bringing Füssli to England was Sir Andrew Mitchell, the ambassador to the court of Frederick the Great. Mitchell has long been overlooked by scholars discussing relations between England and Germany, and he deserves some mention in this connection.

Mitchell attented Leyden university in 1730 and before that he had spent several years in foreign travel. He was an intimate friend of James Thomson, but I have been unable to determine just what connection Mitchell may have had with the Hamburg poets whose poetic affinities with Thomson have often been noted. When Thomson died in 1748 Mitchell was one of his executors. His official relations with Germany began in 1756 when he was appointed ambassador to Frederick at Berlin. Mitchell was acquainted with Gottsched and was well aware of the Gottsched-Lessing controversy. He was also a personal friend of the poet Gellert for whom Mitchell gained an audience with Frederick. Carlyle, in his history of Frederick, states that Mitchell was very active in recommending German literature to the king and often advised him "that a new German literature is springing up, of far more importance than the King thinks." From Carlyle we also learn that Mitchell was active in the Lessing-Gottsched controversy—on the side of Lessing! Carlyle records the following interesting conversation between Gottsched and Mitchell.

> "Genial if you will," said Gottsched, "but the Laws of Aristotle; Five Acts, unities strict!" — "Aristotle? What is to hinder a man from making his tragedy in ten acts if it suit him better?" "Impossible, your Excellency!" — "Pooh," said his Excellency; "suppose Aristotle, and general fashion too, had ordered that the clothes of every man were to be cut from five ells of cloth: "How would the Herr Professor like (with these huge limbs of his) if he found there were no breeches for him on Aristotle's account?"[10]

In 1763 Sir Andrew Mitchell met Heinrich Füssli. Füssli, the godson of the popular poet and painter Salomon Gessner, was educated in his father's home, and among the instructors who taught him were the literary critics of such importance to the development of German literature, Johann Jacob Bodmer and Johann Jacob Breitinger. Other friends of Füssli were Johann Christian Lavater the physiognomist, and Johann Georg Sulzer, the literary and music critic and friend of Klopstock. Bodmer, Breitinger, and Sulzer had been formulating plans to establish active literary connections with England, and Füssli agreed to go to London to help carry out this plan. In 1763 Füssli was introduced by Sulzer to the English ambassador in Berlin, Sir Andrew Mitchell, and Mitchell, who was also actively concerned with this plan to effect closer literary ties between Germany and England, sent Füssli to London with his recommendations and blessings. Mitchell himself came to London early the next year, 1764, and remained until 1766.

In London Füssli found a friend and patron in the banker, Thomas Coutts, and in the publisher Joseph Johnson. Through Johnson, at whose home Füssli was a frequent guest, he became acquainted with many of the leading artists and writers in London. He immediately began to fulfill his duty by translating several very important works by Johann Joachim Winckelmann. These translations form the focal point for one of the most fascinating stories in the history of German-English cultural relations in the eighteenth century. Actually there were four major translations of Winckelmann's writings known in England; two translated by Füssli, a third very probably translated by Füssli, and a French translation reviewed in London.[11]

1. Reflections on the painting and sculpture of the Greeks; with instructions for the connoisseur, and An Essay on Grace in the Works of Art. Translated from the German original of the Abbé Winckelmann, librarian of the Vatican . . . by Henry Fusseli. (London, A. Millar, 1765)

2. A description of the famous marble trunk of Hercules, dug up at Rome, commonly called the Torso of Belvedere; wrought by Apollonius the son of Nestor, and universally allowed to have been made for a statue of Hercules spinning. Translated from the German of the Abbé Winckelmann . . . by Henry Fusle. (London, 1765)

3. Observations on the influence of the different climates upon the polite arts; taken from A history of the fine Arts, by the Abbé Winckelmann, librarian of the Vatican, and antiquary to the Pope. (London, 1765)

4. Histoire de l'art chez les anciens; par M. J. Winckeelmann, président des antiquités a Rome . . . Tr. Robinet. (Amsterdam, 1766).

Thus there appeared in London in two years translations and excerpts of three of Winckelmann's most important works: *Gedanken über die Nachahmung der griechischen Werke in der Malerei und Bildhauerkunst* (1755); *Nachrichten von den neuesten herkulanischen Entdeckungen* (1764); and *Geschichte der Kunst des Altertums* (2 vols. 1764). There also appeared in Glasgow a revised edition of the translation of the *Gedanken über die Nachahmung der griechischen Werke* as: *Reflections concerning the imitation of the Grecian artists in painting and sculpture, in a series of letters*, (Glasgow, R. Urie, 1766). During this time there were also several letters from Rome concerning these translations which were published in London and Glasgow newspapers and periodicals. The primary instigator of this revived and revised Hellenism in London was

Heinrich Füssli. There were, however, others involved in this exchange of ideas. One was the literary, art, and music critic Daniel Webb, who must be woven into this history. B. H. Stern in his *The Rise of Romantic Hellenism in English Literature* (New York, 1940) suggests that by the year 1786 the ideas of Winckelmann were well enough known in England to reappear in most of the histories of Greek art. But why so late, when the primary translations appeared in 1765 and 1766? The apparent answer is that there was even before 1765 a strong interest in Greek art in London, and the suggestion is that many of Winckelmann's ideas were anticipated in the writings of Shaftesbury, Burke, Hogarth, Hume, and Daniel Webb; particularly in Daniel Webb. Five years before the translations of Winckelmann appeared in London Daniel Webb published *An Inquiry into the Beauties of Painting* (London, 1760). This important work was already in a fourth edition in 1777. Webb's *Inquiry* anticipates, almost paraphrases, several of the important ideas from Winckelmann's *Gedanken über die Nachahmung der griechischen Werke* and from Winckelmann's later works written in Rome. The mystery of this striking similarity of thought is solved by a now obscure work published in Zürich, 1766: *Untersuchungen des Schönen in der Mahlerey, aus dem Englischen ins Deutsche übersetzt*. This is a German translation of Daniel Webb's *An Inquiry into the Beauties of Painting*. And in the "Vorrede von H. Füssli"[12] we learn that Daniel Webb and Johann Joachim Winckelmann were personal friends and companions in Rome. From Füssli's description of this friendship we can imagine Webb and Winckelmann strolling, arm in arm, through the ruins and museums of Rome formulating their ideas on the meaning of it all. And thus we see those far reaching ideas of Winckelmann's teacher Oeser being disseminated via Rome by means of Daniel Webb into London art circles, and via Zürich by means of Heinrich Füssli into the same circles.

In 1769 Daniel Webb published *Observations on the Correspondence between Poetry and Music*. This theme was not new in London. The Abbé Du Bos' *Critical Reflections on Poetry, Painting, and Music* had been translated by Thomas Nugent and published in London in 1748. In 1763 John Brown had published his *Dissertation on Poetry and Music*. The line to Germany goes through Johann Georg Sulzer who had been studying the relationships among the arts since 1761, and who finally published his *Allgemeine Theorie der schönen Künste* in 1771-1774. Daniel Webb's *Observations on the Correspondence between Poetry and Music* was translated into German by J. J. Eschenburg and published at Leipzig in 1771, the same year as Sulzer's *Allgemeine Theorie* which contained his important essay on "Ausdruck in der Musik."

The Zürich-London art, music, and literary circle was certainly one of the most important of the intellectual circles of men concerned with

German-English relations. Füssli and Sulzer were personal friends of the poet Klopstock and the artist-poet Salomon Gessner, and both Klopstock and Gessner were translated into English during this same period. Füssli, the pupil of Bodmer and Breitinger, the extollers of Shakespeare, became an important illustrator of scenes from Shakespeare in London. He became President of the Royal Academy. He was teacher and personal friend of William Blake, and the strong similarities of feeling in the art of Füssli and Blake are very evident. This, of course, brings in the thread of pietism-mysticism binding the two cultures. The connecting link in Germany is Gessner, Klopstock, and Sulzer, who was a theologian. It should also be mentioned that Winckelmann himself had been trained in theology at Halle, the site of German Pietism. One could go on, but to do so would be straining the concept of a "survey." The details and significance of these events must yet be filled in, but this brief outline should be sufficient evidence and warning to the future scholar that there is no "pure literature," and that "literary influence" can come from many an unexpected source.

C.   GERMANS IN THE ROYAL SOCIETY

It is both ironic and significant that one of the "founders" of the Royal Society was a German, Theodor Haak. The irony is obvious. The significance lies in the fact that from the time the Society received its royal charter in 1663 German scholars were very influential in its organization, administration, and development. There is also significance in the fact that Haak was not primarily a scientist, but a literary scholar and translator, and had close connections with important English men of letters. It was he who made the first German translation of Milton's *Paradise Lost*.

From the founding of the Royal Society until 1770 there were more than 120 Germans elected to membership. Some of these men were never in England and therefore had little personal contact with English thought and culture, but the fact that their work was sufficiently known and esteemed in England to merit their election to the Royal Society indicates that to the members of the Royal Society at least, Germany was more than a "vast tract of country, overrun with hussars and classical editors." (Stockley, 1) Along with Haak, one of the most influential members of the Society from its founding was the Society's first secretary, Heinrich Oldenburg, a German from Bremen.

In 1665 Oldenburg privately founded a periodical, *The Philosophical Transactions*. Under his guidance this periodical later became the *Transactions of the Royal Society*, and Oldenburg served both as Secretary to the Society and as editor of the *Transactions* until his death in 1677. During that time he issued 136 numbers, thirty-four of which were either written or translated by him. Oldenburg was not a scientist himself, but he was the friend of many scientists and men of letters, and his German background enabled him to obtain contributions for the *Transactions* from many writers on the continent.

Oldenburg's death in 1677 plus the interruption of normal communication between England and France during the wars between those two countries caused discontinuance of the publication of the *Transactions* in 1687. The man who revived the *Transactions*, who served as editor for sixteen years, and who later became President of the Royal Society was, like Theodor Haak and Heinrich Olenburg, a man with strong German connections, Hans Sloane. In 1693 Sloane became Secretary of the Society and to insure the regular publication of the *Transactions* he took over the task of editor himself. Sloane, like Oldenburg, had close contact with many of the scientists on the continent and he continued Oldenburg's policy of inviting foreign contributions. He served as secretary of the Society until 1712 and on Newton's death in 1727 he became President. This was in addition to his duties as President of the College of Physicians and personal physician to George II. As President, Sir Hans Sloane was one of the most influential leaders of the Royal Society and was very active in introducing Germans into membership. In many cases he actually provided for their support while they were in England. In 1723 the Society had created the office of Foreign Secretary and the first person to fill this office was a German, Philip Heinrich Zollmann, appointed by Isaac Newton. Shortly after Sloane's appointment as President in 1727 he expanded the office of Foreign Secretary and appointed two members to this position, both Germans, Johann Kaspar Scheuchzer and Johann Jakob Dillenius. The name of Scheuchzer was not unknown in scientific circles in England. The father of Johann Kaspar, Johann Jakob Scheuchzer, had been elected a Fellow of the Royal Society in 1703 because of his work in natural history, geography, and botany. He was famous for his work on the history and geography of the Alps and this work was later used by Schiller during the writing of *Wilhelm Tell*.[13] Scheuchzer, who, according to Curt von Faber du Faur, was "simultaneously an empirical natural scientist and a Christian who believed in the Bible," (*German Baroque Literature*, [New Haven, 1958], 472) is remembered today for his magnificent ... *Physica Sacra oder Geheiligte Natur-Wissenschafft derer in Heil. Schrift vorkommenden natürlichen Sachen, deutlich erklärt und bewährt* ... , (Augsburg und Ulm, 1731-33).

Scheuchzer's son, Johann Kaspar, had first come to England in 1722 as the personal secretary to Sir Hans Sloane. The fact that Sloane had a German as his personal secretary is indicative of his close ties to that country. In 1724 Scheuchzer was elected a Fellow of the Royal Society and in 1728 was made Foreign Secretary of the Society.

77

During his service as Foreign Secretary he was also active as a physician and wrote a work on the successful inoculation for smallpox. He died quite unexpectedly in Sloane's house in 1729.

Johann Jakob Dillenius, the other Foreign Secretary appointed by Hans Sloane, was studying medicine in Holland in 1721 when he met William Sherard who persuaded him to come to England rather than return to Germany. Dillenius stayed with Sherard at Oxford and with James Sherard, his brother, at London. William Sherard died in 1728 and bequeathed his library and 3000 Pounds to Oxford for the establishment of a professorship of botany on the condition that Dillenius be made the first professor. In 1735 Dillenius was given an M. D. at Oxford, and he received further distinction when Linnaeus commemorated him with the genus *Dillenia* for his work in botany.

Another German who found a patron in Sir Hans Sloane was the naturalist and painter mentioned among the artists, Georg Dyonis Ehret, who did illustrations for the *Transactions*. Sloane was also friendly with the German Moravians who started coming to England in the 1720s, and in 1750 Sloane gave Count Zinzendorf a 99-year lease on Lindsey House, Chelsea, with its terrace and gardens for the use of the *Unitas Fratrum*.

As seen from the example of Haak and Oldenburg, many of the German Fellows of the Royal Society were not primarily scientists. There were German theologians, musicians, artists, and authors as well. Gottfried Wilhelm Leibniz was elected in 1673, and Johann Christian Wolff was elected in 1710. Germans in the Royal Society who are discussed elsewhere are the theologian Anthony Horneck, the composer Johann Christian Pepusch, the artist Georg Dyonis Ehret, the editor Christian Friedrich Weichmann, and the scientist and poet Albrecht von Haller. Two German Fellows who have greatly influenced the development of science but whose work lies beyond the limits of this study are Daniel Gabriel Fahrenheit and Sir William Herschel.

German influence in the Royal Society continued to be evident throughout the century, and much of this influence came directly and indirectly from the German Hanoverians on the throne. An interesting example of this direct influence was through Lord Chesterfield (Philip Dormer Stanhope, fourth Earl of Chesterfield, 1694-1773). He had been Gentleman of the Bedchamber to the king's son George, Prince of Wales, as early as 1715, and in 1728 when the Prince became King George II, Chesterfield became a privy councilor and English Ambassador at the Hague. In 1733 he married Petronilla Melusina von der Schulenburg, the natural daughter of George I by his mistress, Countess Ehrengard Melusina von der Schulenburg, duchess of Kendal. Chesterfield's connections with Germany were further strengthened when his natural son Philip, who spoke German fluently, was appointed "resident at Hamburg" in 1756 and "resident minister at Dresden" in 1764.

A literary "protégé" of Lord Chesterfield was Matthew Maty. Maty, who had been active in London as a publisher, writer, and translator, became Foreign Secretary of the Royal Society in 1762, and in 1765 was appointed Secretary. Through Chesterfield, Maty had close connections with Germany and translated scientific and travel literature from German. His son, Paul Henry Maty, followed in the Father's footsteps. He was first appointed Foreign Secretary to the Royal Society, then Secretary, and in both positions he spent much of his time translating from German. Among the works translated by Paul Henry Maty and published in England was Johann Kaspar Riesbeck's *Travels through Germany, in a series of Letters* (London, 1787), which was one of the important works on Germany before de Staël's *De l' Allemagne*. Paul Henry Maty later edited and published the *New Review*, a literary journal that devoted a great deal of attention to German literature and presented this literature in a very favorable light.

Another direct and very important German contribution to the cultural and literary relations of Germany and England which was the result of the German members in the Royal Society was the publication of the *Acta Germanica: or, the Literary Memoirs of Germany ... Done from the Latin and High Dutch by a Society of Gentlemen*, with the dedication to "Martin Folkes, esq., President, and to the Council and Fellows of the Royal Society of London, for Improving natural knowledge." Volume I of the *Acta Germanica* was first published in serial form in 1741 and then in book form in 1743. Volume II appeared in serial form in 1745 and was likely reprinted in book form also, but I have been unable to locate a copy of the second volume in book form. Each volume of the *Acta Germanica* contained near 100 articles by a variety of authors. An attempt to suggest the "influence" of such a work would be speculative, but the *Acta Germanica* does give an indication of the literary connections and the parallel development of scholarship within the two countries. There are contributions to the *Acta Germanica* from Leibniz, and at least two of his articles are of interest to the student of literary history: "A short sketch of reflections of the originals of nations, chiefly taken from their languages," and "Reflections on knowledge, truth, and ideas."

In summary, it is obvious from this sketch of the Royal Society that German scholars were very active in the Society from the beginning. One of the founders was the German translator of Milton, Theodor Haak. The first Secretary and founder of the *Transactions* was the German scholar and translator Heinrich Oldenburg. The first Foreign Secretary was a German and all of the Foreign Secretaries throughout the century were either Germans themselves or English scholars with very close connections with Germany. And, there were up to the year 1770 over 120 Germans elected to membership. These facts do not seem to substantiate the absurd statement from the *Edinburgh Review* repeated by Mrs. Stockley that "there were probably in London [during this time] as many Persian as German scholars."

V. HAMBURG AND LONDON; AFFINITIES AND RELATIONS

Hamburg was not the only city in Germany that enjoyed close relations with England in the eighteenth century. After 1714 many Englishmen were attracted to Hannover and many Hannoverians were attracted to the English Court in London. Dresden, where Lord Chesterfield's son was ambassador, was another congregating place on the continent for Englishmen, and the establishment of the university at Göttingen by George II brought many English students to this German city. Halle with its Pietism and Zürich with its artists and literary critics both had close connections in London. Hamburg, however, more than any other German city, had enjoyed close political and commercial relations with England since the days of the Hanseatic League, and these relations were still evident throughout the eighteenth century and beyond. In addition to the historical ties, Hamburg was the main literary and cultural center of Germany in the early eighteenth century. It was here that German opera rose to such prominence in the late seventeenth and early eighteenth centuries, and it was here that the "Teutschübende Gesellschaft" was formed in 1715. The "Teutsch-übende Gesellschaft", founded by Johann Albert Fabricius, Barthold Heinrich Brockes, Michael Richey, Johann Ulrich König, and others, became known in 1716 as the "Patriotische Gesellschaft," and in 1724 the publication of *Der Patriot*, one of the important eighteenth-century periodicals, was undertaken by the society with Michael Richey as editor. The *Patriot* became as important and as popular in Germany as its English models, *The Tatler* and *The Spectator* had been in England. The *Republic of Letters* in 1729 printed a eulogy of this German periodical and said that "great masters may sometimes raise disciples to equal themselves."[1]

There were a number of contributing editors to the *Patriot* including Brockes, Fabricius, Christian Friedrich Weichmann, Friedrich von Hagedorn, and Dr. John Thomas, pastor of the English society in

81

Hamburg, and all of these important writers had strong connections with London.

Barthold Heinrich Brockes had enjoyed popularity in London as early as 1716 through his oratorio "Der für die Sünden der Welt gemarterte und sterbende Jesus." Several of the best composers in Hamburg had written music for this oratorio but the most successful was Handel, who first took the oratorio to London. In 1721 Brockes began publishing the work on which his fame still rests, *Irdisches Vergnügen in Gott*. In this large collection of poetry Brockes produced what might be called a poetic complement to the fourth book of Johann Arndt's *Vom wahren Christentum*. Brockes expresses his adoration for the Creator through a joyful appreciation of the creation, and in this sense it is a poetic continuation of the "divine analogy" spoken of in Chapter III. Compare, for example, Arndt's statement on the sun, with a like statement by Brockes. Arndt's prose analogy reads: "If God created so beautiful, refreshing, enlivening, clear, and shining a light; how much more lovely, comfortable, and refreshing a light must *He* be *Himself*?" This is expressed in poetic form by Brockes as follows:

> Edle Quelle güldner Klarheit,
> Deine Grüsse, Kraft und Pracht
> Zeigen uns die grosse Wahrheit,
> Dass der Gott, der dich gemacht,
> Unbeschreiblich schöner, grösser,
> Unaussprechlich heitrer, besser,
> Unbegreiflich herrlicher,
> Höher und gewaltiger.

Another clear example of the analogous nature of Brockes poetry is seen in his comparison of a Biblical passage with a passage from the "Buch der Welt." The poem is called: "Die notwendige Verehrung Gottes in seinen Werken."

> Johannes schreibt: So jemand spricht:
> Ich liebe Gott, und liebt doch seinen Bruder nicht,
> Der ist ein Lügner.
> Denn wer
> Den Bruder, den er siehet,
> Zu lieben nicht wird angetrieben,
> Wie kann er Gott, den er nicht siehet, lieben?

> Im Buch der Welt stehet auch: So jemand spricht:
> Ich ehre Gott, und ehret ihn in den Werken nicht,
> Der ist ein Lügner.
> Denn wer
> Die Werke, die er siehet,
> Nicht einsten würdigt zu betrachten,
> Wie kann der Gott, den er nicht siehet, achten?

In 1745 Brockes translated into German James Thomson's *Seasons*. It is not at all unusual that Brockes should have been attracted to Thomson's work since the *Seasons* is somewhat related in objective and method to the *Irdisches Vergnügen in Gott*. In one of the longer poems from the first part of *Irdisches Vergnügen in Gott* published in 1721, "Die Sonne," Brockes describes in some detail the four seasons of the year by comparing them to a single day; morning is spring, noon summer, afternoon fall, and 'night is winter.

> Wenn des Jahrs verschiedne Zeiten
> Uns verschiedne Pracht bereiten,
> Scheinet jedes Tages Schein
> Auch ein kleines Jahr zu sein

Brockes then proceeds with a brief description of each of the seasons and compares them with the corresponding part of each day. This poem by Brockes is an example of the oft noticed similarities between Brockes and Thomson. The parallel procedure of the two poets is even more striking when one compares Brockes *Irdisches Vergnügen in Gott* as a whole with Thomson's *Seasons* rather than concentrating on one poem such as "Die Sonne."

One of the best statements of Brockes' attitude toward poetry and his purposes in writing *Irdisches Vergnügen in Gott* is given us by Brockes himself. In many ways this statement is an echo of the rationalistic, empirical attitude toward nature, but by reading closely and by comparing Borckes' theories with his practice we can discern a somewhat stronger tendency toward emotionalism and subjectivity than we normally find in the rationalistic philosophy of the early eighteenth century. This fusion of the emotions with reasons is actually an early concept, although unclearly formulated, of the universality of literature as outlined later by Friedrich Schiller, Friedrich Schlegel, and Friedrich Schelling.

> Wenn ich aber gar bald gewahr ward, daß die Poesie, wofern sie keinen sonderlichen und zwar nützlichen Endzweck hätte, ein leeres Wortspiel sei und keine große Hochachtung verdiente, als bemühete ich mich solche Objecte meiner Dichtkunst zu erwählen, woraus die Menschen nebst einer erlaubten Belustigung zugleich erbauet werden möchten. Da ich denn erstlich das bekannte nachher in verschiedene Sprachen übersetzte Passionsoratorium verfertigt, nachgehends aber durch die Schönheit der Natur gerühret, mich entschloß, den Schöpfer derselben in fröhlicher Betrachtung und möglicher Beschreibung zu besingen. Wozu ich mich um so viel mehr verpflichtet hielte, als ich eine so große und fast unverantwortliche Nachlässigkeit, Unempfindlichkeit und den daraus folgenden Undank gegen den allmächtigen Schöpfer für höchst sträflich und den Christenthum ganz unanständig hielte. Verfertigte demnach, zumal der Frühlingszeit verschiedene einzelne Stücke und suchte darin die Schönheit der Natur nach Möglichkeit zu beschreiben, um so wohl mich selbst als andere zu des weisen Schöpfers Ruhme durch eigenes Vergnügen je mehr und mehr anzufrischen. (*ADB* Article on Brockes by Redlich).

The chronology and development of this concept formulated by Brockes with reference to his oratorio of 1712 is important to understand in order to avoid the misconception that has trapped so many scholars aware of the parallels and similarities between Brockes and Thomson. In his book, *German Influences in the English Romantic Period*, F. W. Stokoe has said of English poetry in the early eighteenth century:

> Over England, indeed, was showing the unpromising dawn of a new era in the "Nature" poetry of Thomson, Collins, Gray, in the subjective effusions of Young; and Germany, in reflecting the faint gleam, did something to disperse its own darkness and torpor, to shake off the incubus of French classical and pseudo-classical formalism. (2)

The importance of this English "Nature" poetry has never been denied, but the above statement is quite misleading in that it overlooks Brockes, Günther, and the entire German background of nature poetry and "subject effusions" already well established. This mistake by Stokoe is either the result of an unfamiliarity with the German poetry of the time or a lack of concern with chronological, historical facts. The greatest poet of the early eighteenth century in Germany to display these "subjective effusions" spoken of was Johann Christian Günther (1695-1723) who had great influence on the *Sturm und Drang* poets of the later part of the century. The most influential of the "nature" poets in Germany at this time was undoubtedly Brockes. Some of the later poets in Germany who acknowledged the influence of Brockes in their own poetry were Bodmer, Haller, Gessner, Wieland, and, one of the greatest of German lyric poets, Eduard Mörike.

Mrs. Stockley, in her book *German Literature as known in England 1750-1830*, has been more specific in her discussion of this nature poetry. Observing the reviews and notices of German literature in English periodicals she writes:

> The magazines of the time, though replete with notices of German philosophical, theological, legal and scientific works, contain but one review of a work, purely literary in character, i.e. Brocke's [sic] Irdisches Vergnügen in Gott (1748) [sic], an imitation of Thomson's *Seasons*. (15)

The anachronism committed here has led to an erroneous conclusion. Brockes' translation of Thomson's *Seasons* was published in 1745. Mrs. Stockley was evidently not aware that Brockes' 1748 publication, following the translation of the *Seasons*, was the "neunter und letzter Theil" of a work that Brockes had begun almost thirty years earlier. Mrs. Stockley cites George M. Baker, who also calls the *Irdisches Vergnügen in Gott* an imitation of Thomson's *Seasons*, as an authority for this mistake."[2] Even the literary historian Fritz Schmidt who knew the correct chronology of the two works in question could not avoid the common misconception that Brockes' work was the result of a "Wirkung von Pope und Thomson."[3] And, once an error in literary history becomes a cliché, it is very difficult for even the trained historian to avoid it. Consequently we find even in René Wellek's *A History of Modern Criticism* (New Haven, 1955) a statement on "the enormous success of Thomson's *Seasons* in Germany with such imitators as Brockes, Haller, and Ewald von Kleist." (I, 161) A careful look at the chronology will clear up the misunderstanding, and we will then be in a better position to consider the significance of the parallel development of nature poetry as reflected in Thomson and Brockes.

Brockes (1680-1747) began publishing poetry when Thomson (1700-1748) was five years old. The idea that poetry without a "nützlichen Endzweck" was "ein leeres Wortspiel... und keine große Hochachtung verdiente" was incorporated by Brockes in his oratorio in 1712, and his decision "den Schöpfer... in fröhlicher Betrachtung und möglicher Beschreibung zu besingen" resulted in the publication of the first part of *Irdisches Vergnügen in Gott* in 1721, five years before Thomson published the first part of the *Seasons*. The chronology of Brockes *Irdisches Vergnügen in Gott* and Thomson's *Seasons* is as follows:

1721 – *Irdisches Vergnügen in Gott* I

1724 – *Irdisches Vergnügen in Gott* I,   2nd edition

1726 – *Irdisches Vergnügen in Gott* I,   3rd edition
       – *Winter*

1727 – *Irdisches Vergnügen in Gott* II
       – *Irdisches Vergnügen in Gott* I,   4th edition
       – *Summer*

1728 – *Irdisches Vergnügen in Gott* III
       – *Spring*

1730 – *Irdisches Vergnügen in Gott* II,   2nd edition
       – *Irdisches Vergnügen in Gott* III, 2nd edition
       – *Autumn*
       – Complete *Seasons*

Perhaps the most appropriate summary to this discussion of Brockes and Thomson has been given by Harold Jantz:

> Just how a work published in 1721 could be influenced by a work published in 1726, critics and historians do not tell us. If they should ever decide to look in the opposite direction (in which everyone knows in advance there could be no movement), they might find something very interesting, but that would compel them to a detailed examination of facts and phenomena, something not at all as delightful and reassuring as the old wind-blown absurdities.[4]

The important matter at hand is not a concern with "influence" so much as it is a concern with the striking parallel development of English and German literature during the early eighteenth century. The poetry of both Brockes and Thomson is in harmony with the rationalistic oriented philosophy that saw God revealed through natural and demonstrable laws, but, paradoxically, there is at least in Brockes' poetry an underlying strain of mysticism, and the influence of Arndt's *Vom wahren Christentum* is unmistakable. A chronologically closer source of philosophical inspiration for Brockes was Leibniz' *Theodicee* which appeared in 1710, just at the formative stage in Brockes' poetic thought, and the *Theodizee*, both as a particular and as a type, represents the element of the Enlightenment in Brockes' poetry. The Pietistic, emotional, mystic element in this poetry is more intangible, but certainly grew out of his educational background at Halle and the general Pietistic environment of the times.

A man who was less of a poet but who had more direct relations with England was Christian Friedrich Weichmann, editor of the first two volumes of *Poesie der Niedersachsen*, and contributor to *Der Patriot*. He was very closely associated with the members of the Hamburg literary circle including the two Englishmen John Thomas and Thomas Lediard, who will be discussed later. Weichmann dedicated the first volume of *Poesie der Niedersachsen* (1721) to his friend Brockes, and the second volume (1723) to the editor of the *Patriot*, Michael Richey.

Some time after the publication of the *Poesie der Niedersachsen* Weichmann went to England. The 1729 edition of the *Patriot* lists the contributing editors and speaks of Weichmann as a "Königlicher Gesellschaft in London Mitgliede." The German painter Balthasar Denner, who was a close friend of Brockes, Hagedorn, Weichmann, and others of the Hamburg circle, was in England from 1721 to 1725, and after a short stay in Hamburg he returned to England from 1726 to 1728. There is a portrait of Christian Weichmann by Denner in the Bodleian library, and this painting was probably done while they were both in England. Weichmann was granted a degree at Oxford and in 1728 he was elected a Fellow of the Royal Society. With such strong connections in both countries, Weichmann was one of the important intermediaries between Germany and England in the early part of the century.

The major English representative of the Hamburg literary circle was Bishop John Thomas who went to Hamburg in 1725 to serve as Chaplain for the English society there and did not return until 1734. The *Dictionary of National Biography* states that while in Germany he "published a paper in German called the 'Patriot' in imitation of the 'Spectator.'" The *Patriot* was published, of course, by Michael Richey, but it is true that John Thomas was a contributing editor as has been mentioned. Thomas was apparently well pleased with his associations in the Hamburg literary circle and with his position as Chaplain of the English merchants in Hamburg, and therefore he declined an offer from George I for preferment in England. He maintained his connections with England, however, and in 1728 he received a D.D. degree from Cambridge while still serving as Chaplain in Hamburg. The publication of the *Patriot* was discontinued in 1726, but Thomas remained in Hamburg for another eight years. Bishop Thomas Newton has described the manner of his eventual return to England.

> Dr. Thomas was accustomed, as well as Dr. Lockyer his predecessor in the chaplainship at Hamburg to go from Hamburg to pay his duty at Hannover every year that the King came over. After some time the King (George II) asked him, whether if he could obtain any preferment from the crown, he would not gladly leave Hamburg to settle in England? He replied that his Majesty's father had made him the like gracious offer, and he had declined it . . . but now . . . he should think himself very happy to return to England under his Majesty's patronage and protection.[5]

In 1736 Thomas returned to Germany for a short stay as the King's personal Chaplain. His close friendship with George II was due in some measure to his ability to converse with the King in German, and to his affiliations with the *Patriot* and the Hamburg poets.

A good friend of Bishop Thomas at the court was John Carteret, Earl of Granville. Carteret was also very close to the King because of his ability to speak fluent German. He was appointed Prime Minister in 1746, but being unable to form a ministry he resigned from what he jokingly called the administration of "48 hours, 7 minutes, and 11 seconds," now spoken of as the "short administration." Carteret was at one time Lord Lieutenant of Ireland where he had an acquaintance with Jonathan Swift.

Another link in the Hamburg-London chain was Friedrich von Hagedorn. Hagedorn contributed articles to the *Patriot* and poems to Weichmann's *Poesie der Niedersachsen* before he published his own *Versuch einiger Gedichte* in 1729. Later in 1729 Hagedorn went to England as Secretary to the Danish ambassador in London and remained there until 1731. In 1733 he again went to England, this time as Secretary for a trade organization at the English court, and his English connections were substantially strengthened when he married the daughter of an English merchant living in Hamburg.

Hagedorn is usually spoken of as a Rococo poet, and there has been much written showing the importance of English literature in forming and molding his literary style. In order to emphasize the English influence on Hagedorn, Bertha Reed Coffman tries to minimize the significance of Hagedorn's poetic concepts before his first trip to England in 1729.[6] In doing so, however, Mrs. Coffman failed to see that the critical attitudes in the "Vorrede" to Hagedorn's *Versuch einiger Gedichte* are of the same type as the attitudes that inspired the *Sturm und Drang*.[7]

F. W. Stokoe, probably not familiar at all with Hagedorn's *Versuch einiger Gedichte*, made the same mistakes as Mrs. Coffman when he stated that Germany "did something to disperse its own darkness and torpor" by reflecting "the subjective effusions of Young." (2) Certainly Young's *Conjectures on Original Composition* (1759) and *The Complaint; or Night Thoughts on Life, Death, and Immortality* (1742) were very important in both England and Germany. It should not be overlooked, however, as it has been by Mrs. Coffman and F. W. Stokoe, that these "subjective effusions" and the concept of poetic inspiration and originality were expressed as early as 1729 by Hagedorn.

In the "Vorrede" to his *Versuch einiger Gedichte* he speaks of fire, enthusiasm, inspiration, and a disdain for rules. The unanswerable question is how much of what Hagedorn later called his "jugendliche Übereilung" was spread from Hagedorn to other critics and associates in Hamburg and London. Three years before the publication of *Versuch einiger Gedichte* Hagedorn expressed many of his radical ideas about poetry to Christian Weichmann. In a letter from Hagedorn to Weichmann dated 25 October, 1726 (Hagedorn was eighteen years old) he speaks about his reluctance to destroy the spirit of his poetry by revisions and improvements (Weichmann was his editor at that time), and he concludes that "das viele Ausbessern demjenigen lebhaften Feuer, worauf das Salz und die Höhe der Gedanken beruht, oft mehr schadet als nutzet." And Hagedorn could not understand "wie die muntre Lebhaftigkeit eines feurigen Geistes mit der weichherzigen Furcht eines kleingläubigen Sylbenzerrers sich vergleichen lasse." These views had not changed by 1729, but had grown stronger and clearer in Hagedorn's mind. He speaks of the desirability of uniting youthful fire with mature judgment, and nature with art.

> Die Anmuht mit der Tiefsinnigkeit, das Feuer mit der Ordnung und Reiffe, die Schönheit wohlgewälter Worte mit der Schönheit neuer Gedancken, die Natur mit der Kunst zu verbinden, und hiebey Abwege und Ausschweiffungen zu vermeiden, schiene mir jederzeit nichts geringes, und meine Eigen-Liebe war nie leichtgläubig genug, um sich mit der süssen Einbildung zu schmeicheln, daß ich diese Stuffen würcklich beschreiten können.[8]

He talks about the futility of attempting to apply rules to beauty and he speaks of uninhibited freedom of expression.

> Von dem eigentlichen Wesen der Schönheit lassen sich keine durchgängige Regeln geben. Es zeiget sich von selbst, und gefällt, so bald es sich gezeiget. Es ist verwegen, mit kaltsinnigem Gemüht, mit einer schläfrigen Unempfindlichkeit von Wercken zu urtheilen, die mit aufgewecktem Geiste geschrieben worden. Das Leben einer Ode bestehet, wo ich nicht irre, in dem starcken Feuer, welchem eine ungebundene Freyheit die beste Nahrung ertheilet.

Hagedorn's description of the workings of a poet's mind could have been written by Maximilian Klinger or Johann Gottfried Herder in the midst of the *Sturm und Drang* enthusiasm. The entire "Vorrede" reveals a type of critical expression hardly expected in 1729. Just how widespread these startling ideas were is hard to determine.

Hagedorn discussed them with Christian Weichmann before Weichmann went to England, and it is likely that he discussed them with other members of the Hamburg circle. Hagedorn was in England himself the same year that his *Versuch einiger Gedichte* was published, and he remained there two years. An echo of these ideas apeared in Salomon Gessner's *Tod Abels* (1758), and Gessner had just previously made a special trip to Hamburg to meet Hagedorn. Further research should make it more obvious that much of the critical attitude of the *Sturm und Drang* was actually well established and formulated in German culture by this circle of Hamburg poets.

One of the most fascinating persons in Hamburg connected with German-English cultural relations was Thomas Lediard, Secretary to the English Ambassador at Hamburg from 1713 until 1732. On the title page of Nathan Bailey's *Dictionarium Britannicum . . . the second edition . . . assisted by T. Lediard* (London, 1736), Lediard describes himself as a "professor of modern languages in Lower Saxony," and in addition to these duties he wrote and produced operas, wrote histories, and translated from German to English. He was a friend of John Thomas and was also acquainted with the other members of the Hamburg literary circle and editors of the *Patriot*. In 1725 Lediard made a contribution to the literary ties between Germany and England by publishing *Grammatica Anglicana Critica, oder Versuch zu einer vollkommen Grammatic der englischen Sprache*. In 1732 he returned to England and in the same year his opera *Brittania* was set to music by the German composer Johann Friedrich Lampe and performed at the Haymarket theater. In 1735 he began his career as historian and rapidly wrote *The Naval History of England* (1735), *The Life of John, Duke of Marlborough* (1736), and *The History of the Reigns of William III and Mary, and Anne* (1737). He then began his career as translator and published in 1737 his most well-known translation, Johann Jacob Mascov's *History of the Ancient Germans*. The translation appeared in two large octavo volumes and was dedicated "to the noble and right honourable, Sir Robert Walpole." Among the many subscribers are listed the Earl of Chesterfield, James Oglethorp, Mr. Pepusch, Mons. le Comte de Sinzendorff, [sic] Sir Hans Sloane, and Sir Cyr. Wich, all of whom had German connections. Lediard continued his work as translator and published J. B. Fischer's *A Plan of Civil and Historical Architecture*. Also in 1738 he published his most famous literary work, *The German Spy*.

This book was advertised on the title page as being "written by a Gentleman on his Travels, to his Friend in England, With a Prefatory Account of these Letters, and Explanatory Notes, by Thomas Lediard, Esq." The whole work is probably by Lediard, however, and derived from Lediard's own experiences in Germany and from his fertile imagination. Lediard displays great skill in remaining anonymous without making himself obscure. One of the reasons for remaining anonymous must have been to praise his own stage productions in Hamburg without sounding too vain. This whole episode is delightfully done. The "Gentleman on his Travels" praises the elaborate and beautiful production of "Mr. L——d," but in order to prevent the praise from sounding too lavish the "Gentleman" (Lediard) concludes his description of the production with a few mild criticisms which the editor of *The German Spy* (Lediard) rebutts in a footnote, and thereby commends himself twice.

> These pieces were continued for four successive days, and met with the applause they justly deserv'd: But this I must beg leave to observe, that tho' my friend, Mr. L——d, has, upon this occasion, shewn a great fertility of invention, yet it borders too much on that false wit so beautifully describ'd by Mr. Addison, in the first volume of the Spectators, and abounds too much in Chronograms and the like.

At this point the editor inserts a note: "This censure of the author's is, beyond all dispute, very just, but then he should have consider'd, that these inventions were for the entertainment of Germans, who are far from thinking them false wit." This is also a clever way to point out the changing concepts of dramatic art in Germany and England at that time. The letter of the "Gentleman" continues: "So likewise his architecture, tho' very beautiful, has a little too much of the Gothick in it, I mean of the extravagances of an irregular fancy." The editor adds another note and takes the opportunity to advertise another of his books.

> Here I must beg leave to dissent from our author: The architecture was not, indeed, perfectly modern, and it would have been ridiculous if it had; as the representation was that of an ancient Heathen Temple. If the author, who ever he be, will give himself the trouble of looking into the volume I have published of the theatrical representations of my invention, he may perhaps find I am not quite a stranger to modern architecture.[9]

In Chapter XII of *The German Spy* Lediard describes the opera house in Hamburg and comments on the great success of a performance of Handel's *Julius Caesar* which Lediard had translated into German. He discusses his preference for the German opera over the Italian opera, and his comments on a tragic opera by Telemann are important for an understanding of the development of the opera in Hamburg at this time, and for an exemplification of the censure of the Italian opera being voiced in both Germany and England.

> The words of this opera were not, as generally with us, a mere dead letter, or vehicle to convey the music to our ears; the passions seemed to be finely wrought up in the poetry, and as naturally express'd in the music, a thing seldom or never regarded in the Italian opera.

After describing the tender final scene Lediard concludes:

> To me, I must own, this single scene was worth more, than a whole lifeless Italian

Opera; nor do I think it possible for the utmost skill of the poet, to raise the passions to such a height, as this skiful combination of poetry and music can effect. (98,99)

These remarks on the opera are quite central to the changing concept of drama as it developed in the opera. Much of the controversy carried on by Gottsched and Lessing had its origins in the dispute concerning the place of the opera as a dramatic work of art.

> What! some might be apt to say, give the preference to music set to words, which are a perfect contradiction to music, and sufficient to destroy all harmony: But even this is a vulgar error; the High German is no such disharmonious language, but what a skilful poet, who knows any thing of music, may find words as proper to be set to it as in Italian: And I defy any Italian to point out to me harsher sounds in the German, than I will shew him in his mother tongue. (100)

This statement which is an echo of many passages from the *Patriot* anticipates much that was to be made programatic by Lessing, and these ideas published in England by Lediard are in the spirit of the Hamburg poets whom he knew so well. In the preface to *The German Spy* Lediard says:

> And here I must beg leave to do justice (and to desire you, if you should publish these letters, to do the same) to a society of gentlemen, for whom I, and every one who knows them, must posess the highest esteem: I mean the authors of the *Patriot*, a weekly paper publish'd in Hamburg, in Imitation of our incomparable Spectators, and which is allow'd, by all good judges, to come up the nearest to the spirit of those great originals, of any thing that has been publish'd of that nature.

Lediard also stated in the preface that much of the material in *The German Spy* was suggested to him by certain ideas from the *Patriot*.

CONCLUSION

The literary spirit in Hamburg in the 1720s and 1730s was forward looking. It was still steeped in the Baroque tradition and was filled with the contemporary atmosphere and philosophy of the Enlightenment, but this spirit in Hamburg, more than elsewhere in Germany (and perhaps in Europe) displayed signs of individual genius and subjective intellectualism that were quite different from the ideal, universal type found in the Neo-classicism and Deism of both England and Germany. There was a reaction against these ideas in both countries. The religious reaction has been outlined in Chapter III. The literary-critical reaction is generally thought to have occurred much later, but a fresh look at the literature and criticism coming from these Hamburg-London affiliations will reveal, in embryo at least, most of the prominent ideas that radically changed the direction of literature later in the century. It is no mere coincidence that the two great Shakespeare critics of the century, Lessing and Johnson, both expressed their attitude toward drama in almost identical terms. A cursory reading of Lessing's famous seventeenth "Literaturbrief" (1759) and Johnson's "Preface" to his edition of Shakespeare (1765) will make this similarity evident. Both used Voltaire as their point of departure, both used Addison's *Cato* as the example of what should not be done in drama, and both used Shakespeare's *Othello* as the example of the great drama.

When Lessing said "Look to England" everyone did. In pointing out the English spirit that enkindled the *Sturm und Drang*, however, scholars have often failed to realize that the rapid assimilation of this spirit by German writers came about not because the *Sturm und Drang* poets felt a new spirit, but because these poets recognized a familiar spirit that had been continually stirring just beneath the surface of the Gottsched pseudoclassicism and that had for some time been waiting for great voices like Lessing and Herder to make it more articulate.

VI. "THE GERMAN STORIES,"
WITH EMPHASIS ON SALOMON GESSNER

One of the interesting paradoxes of the German-English cultural relations in the eighteenth century is that Pietism, a German movement, became a more influential social phenomenon in England (and in America) through the "Great Awakening" than in Germany. This situation is clearly illustrated by the visit of the great Pre-romantic critic Johann Georg Hamann to London in 1758. In London he perceived a spiritual force he had not found in Germany. Writing on the hymn, and comparing Johannes Scheffler's "Liebe, die du mich zum Bilde deiner Gottheit hast gemacht" with Edward Young's *Night Thoughts* Hamann says:

> Gott hat eben die Liebe für jeden einzelnen Menschen, die er für das ganze Geschlecht derselben gehabt hat, weil jeder einzelne Mensch Sein Bild in der Schöpfung erhielt. Das Bild deiner Gottheit aber, o Liebe! ist allein durch den Glauben wiederhergestellt, der die Gnade Gottes des Vaters, die Liebe des Sohnes und die Gemeinschaft oder den vertrauten Umgang des heiligen Geistes, in unseren Seelen vereinigt.[1]

The remarks quoted here are born of the same spirit that moved John Wesley to exclaim, about his experience at the meeting in Aldersgate street: "I felt I did trust in Christ, Christ alone, for salvation; and an assurance was given me, that he had taken away *my* sins, even *mine*, and saved *me* from the law of sin and death." The spirit in Hamann as seen from his discussion of Scheffler's hymn, and this same spirit in John Wesley, typifies the emotional and religious atmosphere Hamann found in England—an atmosphere he had not found in his native Germany. John Wesley had learned the doctrine of immediate conversion by faith and grace from his German Moravian teachers. Why is it then, that twenty years later Hamann, an intelligent and very perceptive German, had to come to London to discover the spiritual movement that had originated in Germany?

By examining the major causes of this paradox Hamann's situation becomes clear, and through an understanding of this experience of Hamann's one of the basic configurations of the English-German relations in the eighteenth century becomes clear also. The particular configuration is actually a circular pattern of influence from Germany to England in the first half of the century and from England to Germany beginning near the middle of the century.

Philip Jakob Spener's *Collegia pietatis* was organized in 1670 and was soon established at the new university at Halle which became the physical and spiritual center for the movement known as Pietism. Halle Pietism reached its great strength and popularity in the first decades of the eighteenth century and it was at this time that such strong connections were established with London through Prince George, Heinrich Wilhelm Ludolf, Johan Christian Jacobi, Anton Wilhelm Boehm, and others. Contemporary with this movement was the development of a rationalistic theology and an empirical philosophy which soon made their influence felt even in German Pietistic circles, and when August Gottlieb Spangenberg went to Halle in 1732 as a professor of religious education, expecting to find an atmosphere of religious liberality, he found instead a dry and spiritless authoritarian system of dogma, and a year later he was dismissed from his position at Halle for adhering to the concepts that had given Pietism its birth. Spangenberg had to go to Herrnhut to find the spiritual enthusiasm he was seeking.

Pietism arrived in England from Halle, and shortly after it reached its greatest strength in "The Society for the Propagation of the Gospel in Foreign Parts" and its greatest popularity marked by the second English edition of *Vom wahren Christentum* (1720), George Berkeley was already denying the material supports for Locke's empirical theories and Hume's scepticism was becoming more and more audible. James Thomson was writing poetry which was rationalistic, but with emotional overtones. All this, however, might not have saved the spirit of Halle Pietism in England from the fate it suffered in Germany had it not been for the sweet singing of the Moravians. John Wesley confessed that he went to America to convert the Indians but soon discovered he was not converted himself. The Moravians were able to rekindle this spirit of conversion. The question now is, why did Hamann have to come to London to find this spirit?

Moravian emotional excesses and strange practices had made their brand of Pietism appear ridiculous and repulsive to many people in Germany and England who might otherwise have been attracted to it. In England, however, this brand of Pietism found a practical patron in John Wesley, who was able to root out the tares without destroying the wheat; that is, he had the real ability to see the spiritual strength of the movement without being emotionally overwhelmed by it. Thus what remained a minor movement in Germany turned

94

into one of the most wide-spread and influential religious revivals in England since the Reformation. The other reason Hamann had not found this spirit in Germany is that Herrnhut was neither Hamburg nor Berlin, that is, it was not a cultural center. The English Herrnhut, however, was London, the very center of cultural activity.

The religious atmosphere in London was, of course, more than transplanted Pietism. A real synthesis had taken place, and Hamann found the English counterpart of this synthesis in such poets as Edward Young, whose *Night Thoughts* were discussed in Hamann's "Betrachtungen zu Kirchenliedern" alongside Johannes Scheffler's mystical hymns. The type of imagery Hamann found in the *Night Thoughts* further reveals the German-English synthesis.

> ... O thou bleeding Love!
> Thou maker of new morals to mankind!
> The grand morality is Love of Thee.

Hamann's somewhat embellished translation is:

> O du blutende Liebe!
> Du Schöpfer neuer Sittenlehren für die Menschen!
> Der Grundstein und der Gipfel der erhabensten Sittlichkeit
> Ist Dich zu lieben; ist deine Liebe.

This type of imagery came from Paul Gerhardt's "O Haupt voll Blut und Wunden," from the hymns of the German mystics and Pietists and from Johann Arndt's *True Christianity*. This imagery was taken further with Zinzendorf's "blood and wounds hymns," and perhaps reached its climax with William Cowper's:

> There is a fountain filled with blood
> Drawn from Emmanuel's veins;
> And sinners plunged beneath that flood
> Lose all their guilty stains.

In résumé, by the time Hamann reached England in 1758 there had taken place a general synthesis of German and English spiritual thought. The Moravians were at the height of their popularity in England, and Wesley's Methodism, having grown out of the same seed, had become so extensive that it was being discussed as something apart from the Church of England (much to Wesley's dismay). German hymns were found in dozens of collections also containing English hymns, and who could say whether this or that hymn was written by Charles Wesley or translated from German by his brother John?[2] There were more than 5,000 Germans and more than half a dozen German churches in London. William Law and John Byrom had spread the doctrines of Tauler and Jacob Boehme far and wide. Religious leaders such as Law, Byrom, Wesley, and Zinzendorf were among the most popular men in England. Pietism was no longer restricted to the lower classes or to the uneducated. Dr. Johnson only regreted that John Wesley was too busy to stay longer when he came to call. It is not so strange then, that Hamann did not recognize this atmosphere as being German-inspired, but felt that he was in a new world, and the results of this experience in Hamann's life were of such a significant nature that Josef Nadler has been able to say with some accuracy: "Mit diesem Londoner Erlebnis Hamanns ist das neue geistige Deutschland seines Jahrhunderts geboren worden."[3]

Perhaps one of the explanations for the rise of a new spiritual Germany and for the enthusiastic reception of English thought in Germany about this time is that Germany was receiving an English thought tempered with a spirit out of Germany's own past—but a spirit that had undergone such a change in its foreign environment that it was not recognized as being of native extraction.

This concept of the cultural relations between Germany and England make much more understandable the sudden popularity of a certain type of German literature in England known as "The German stories:"[4] Gessner's *Death of Abel*, Rambach's *Pious Aspirations*, Bogatzky's *Edifying Thoughts on God's Paternal Heart*, and *A Golden Treasury for the Children of God*, Rabener's *Employment of Souls after Separation from the Body, a Dream*, Klopstock's *Messiah*, and *Death of Adam*, Rambach's *Meditations . . . on the Sufferings of our Lord and Saviour Jesus Christ*, Wieland's *Trial of Abraham*, Bodmer's *Noah*,—all of which were translated between 1760 and 1770. The atmosphere had been well prepared for this type of literature, and these translations blended immediately into the cultural pattern.

The first and most important specimen of this type of literature to appear in England at this time was Salomon Gessner's *Death of Abel*, translated by Mary Collyer and published in London in 1761. Gessner was immediately popular. The next year three different translations of his *Idylls* were published in London, two anonymously, the third a verse translation by Anne Penny. In the preface to her *Select Poems from M. Gessner's Pastorals* Anne Penny praises Gessner's style, which she calls "a kind of poetic prose," and says that "she was induced to imagine their charms would not be diminished by the decoration of verse." She allows her readers to judge whether or not she has done justice to Gessner's prose style with her verse, and "the only merit she claims is the choice of her authors, as perhaps there have never appeared, in Germany or England, persons of a more refined sentimental turn of writing than the two gentlemen from whose works she has presumed to select subjects for her versification." [Gessner and Johnson] As far as her reading public was concerned she succeeded very well, and her translation of Gessner's *Pastorals* went through at least two editions the first year.[5] In 1762 the second edition of Mary Collyer's translation of *The Death of Abel* was published

96

in London, and editions were published in Boston and Philadelphia the same year. In 1763 it was translated into verse "in the style of Milton" by the Reverend Thomas Newcombe. By 1765 *The Death of Abel* was in its seventh edition, by 1766 it was in its eleventh edition, and by the end of the century more than twenty recorded editions of the Collyer translation had been published, not counting the many reprints.

Mary Collyer had such success with Gessner that she attempted a translation of Klopstock's *Messiah*. She died before the translation was completed, however, and it was continued by her husband Joseph Collyer who published the first ten cantos in 1763. There has been a great deal of controversy over this translation, and many critics have attempted to discover why the *Messiah* did not enjoy the popularity of *The Death of Abel* in view of the fact that Klopstock was hailed as "the German Milton." A partial answer is that in translating Gessner's *Death of Abel* Mrs. Collyer is working with prose whereas her translation of Klopstock's *Messiah* is a prose rendition of a verse epic. The other answer is a denial of the assumption. The fact is that the *Messiah* was not as unpopular in London as some critics have maintained.

I can not completely agree with Professor Morgan's statement in his *Bibliography of German Literature in English Translation* that Mrs. Collyer's translation of *The Death of Abel* is an "imitation rather than a translation," and I am puzzled by his statement that this translation was not acknowledged by Mrs. Collyer until 1786. In describing the 1786 edition he says that it was "the first British edition to name the translator." I have before me the first English edition of 1761. Following the title page is a dedication "to the Queen" which begins: "Madam, permit me to lay at the foot of your Throne this volume which is an attempt to translate from your native language a work deservedly admired." The dedication is signed: "your's and His Majesty's most dutiful, most devoted, and most obedient subject and servant, Mary Collyer." The introductory material also contains a "Translator's Preface" in which Mrs. Collyer defends her translation and concludes: "Such as it is I leave to the candor of the reader, believing, that . . . no one will . . . condemn the assiduous efforts of a female pen." Evidently the translation that Professor Morgan describes did not contain this heart-rending plea for the critic's mercy nor the signed dedication to the Queen in which Mrs. Collyer explains her motives for turning to literary work:

> Placed by the hand of Providence at an humble distance from the Great, my cares and pleasures are concentred within the narrow limits of my little family, and it is in order to contribute to the support and education of my children, I have taken up the pen.

Had Professor Morgan's copy contained these prefaces, he would never have had the heart to give Mrs. Collyer the dagger sign (†) which he says "is comparable to the inverted thumb."

The following quotations from the first lines of Book I of *The Death of Abel* are a sample of Mrs. Collyer's abilities as a translator. The rhythms of Gessner's style which she calls "a kind of loose poetry" are primarily dactylic rhythms.

> Ein erhabnes Lied möchte ich itzt singen, die Haushaltung der Erstgeschaffenen nach dem traurigen Fall, und den ersten, der seinen Staub der Erde wieder gab, der durch die Wuth seines Bruders fiel. Ruhe du itzt, sanfte ländlische Flöte, auf der ich sonst die gefällige Einfalt und die Sitten des Landmanns sang. Stehe du mir bey, Muse, oder edle Begeisterung, die du des Dichters Seele erfüllest, wenn er in stiller Einsamkeit staunt, bey nächtlichen Stunden, wenn der Mond über ihm leuchtet, oder im Dunkeln des Hains, oder bey der einsam beschatteten Quelle. Wenn dann die heilige Entzückung seiner Seele sich bemächtigt, dann schwingt sich die Einbildungskraft erhitzt empor, und fliegt mit kühnen Schwingen durch die geistige und die sichtbare Natur hin, bis ins fernere Reiche des Möglichen, sie spüret das überraschende Wunderbare auf, und das verborgenste Schöne.

Here is Mrs. Collyer's translation. It will be noted that Gessner's dactylic rhythms have become more dominantly iambic.

> Henceforth repose in silence, thou soft pipe, no more I render thee vocal, no more I chant the simple manners of the rustic swain. I would raise my voice to bolder strains, and in harmonious lays rehearse the adventures of our primeval parents after their dreadful fall, I would celebrate him, who, sacrificed by a brother's fury, his dust first mingled with the earth. Come thou noble enthusiasm that warm'st and fillest the mind of the wrapt poet, who during the silent hours of night comtemplates in the thick grove, or at the side of a clear stream, enlighten'd by the moon's pale lamp: seiz'd by a Divine transport, imagination takes her flight, and with bold wing traversing the regions of created substances, penetrates into the distant empire of possibilities, discovering with clear view the marvelous that captivates, and the beautiful that inchants.

The tremendous popularity of Gessner's *Death of Abel* in England is revealing of the tastes of the reading public during this period.

Following, for comparison, are the first lines of Klopstock's *Messiah* and the Collyer translation of 1766.

> Sing, unsterbliche Seele, der sündigen Menschen Erlösung, Die der Messias auf Erden in seiner Menschheit vollendet, Und durch die er Adams Geschlechte die Liebe der Gottheit Mit dem Blute des heiligen Bundes von neuem geschenkt hat. Also geschah des Ewigen Wille. Vergebens erhub sich Satan wider den göttlichen Sohn; umsonst stand Judäa Wider ihn auf; er thats, und vollbrachte die große Versöhnung.

The Collyer translation:

> Inspir'd by thine immortality, rise my soul, and sing the honours of thy great Reedeemer: honours obtain'd in hard adversity's rough school—obtain'd by suffering for the sins and woes of others, himself sinless. Recount, with humble gratitude, those guiltless sufferings, the bitter consequences of love to man's degenerate race. In vain Satan rag'd against the Lord's Anointed: In vain Judea

set herself against him; he accomplish'd, in his humanity the great work of our redemption.

In spite of this prose translation, *The Messiah* did have readers and was not as unpopular as has been thought. The first translation was published in 1763. Professor Morgan lists further editions of the Collyer translation in 1769, 1788, 1795, and 1808, before the verse translations of Egestorff and others began to appear. I have found one edition that has been overlooked. *The Messiah. Attempted from the German of Mr. Klopstock. To which is prefix'd his Introduction on Divine Poetry. The Second Edition* . . . London, 1766. The translation was published in two volumes and the dedication is signed "Joseph Collyer." The importance of this edition and the significance of its unfortunate ommission from Professor Morgan's *Bibliography* is that it was published in 1766. This means that instead of six years between the first and second editions, there were only three years, and there were three editions of *The Messiah* between 1763 and 1769.

In the translation of Klopstock's *Death of Adam* the reverse procedure was used, that is, Robert Lloyd translated Klopstock's prose into verse. I have not seen this translation, but Professor Morgan says it is not too close to the original and that it is "rather flowery and high-flown." When Coleridge visited Klopstock years later Klopstock was still complaining bitterly about the bad treatment he had received at the hands of his English translators.

On the last page of the 1766 edition of Collyer's translation of *The Messiah* is an advertisement for others of his translations:

> Speedily will be publish'd by Jos. Collyer . . . and the booksellers who publish this work, NOAH. In twelve Books. Attempted from the German of Mr. Bodmer. Where may be had, Dedicated to the Queen, the seventh edition of The Death of Abel, attempted from the German of Mr. Gessner.

The promised translation of Bodmer's *Noah* was published in both London and Dublin in 1767, and a second edition appeared in London in 1770. Unfortunately, Bodmer's verse suffered the same fate as Klopstock's.

The titles of these translations appearing between 1760 and 1770 indicate their subject matter, and the strong Pietistic "Awakening" in England insured great popularity for these Biblical themes—for a time at least. Gessner's *Death of Abel* which has great literary merit in its own right enjoyed a much longer popularity than Klopstock or Bodmer, and Gessner was read and appreciated in England more than any other German writer of this time.

Salomon Gessner was one of the leading figures of the Zürich literary and art circle. He was closely associated with the Zürich poets and critics including Johann Jacob Bodmer and Johann Jacob Breitinger, and he was also personally acquainted with the poets Klopstock and

Hagedorn. He was very close to the artistic Füssli family, and was godfather to Heinrich Füssli who later became President of the Royal Academy. Salomon Gessner was successful in his own right as a poet publisher, and as a landscape artist; as the author of the *Idylls* and *The Death of Abel* he became internationally famous.

Everyone in England read Gessner. There were more than twenty editions of *The Death of Abel* before 1800 and nearly as many editions of his *Idylls,* and there were over 120 reviews of his works in British magazines between 1760 and 1810.[6] The *Eclectic Review* in 1810 wrote: *"The Death of Abel,* during the last half-century, has rivalled the *Pilgrim's Progress* and *Robinson Crusoe* in popularity; and for this there must have been some better cause than the bad taste of its readers."[7] This thought was echoed by the *Quarterly Review* in 1814:

> No book of foreign growth has ever become so popular in England as the *Death of Abel*.... It has been repeatedly printed at country presses, with worn types and on coarse paper, and it is found at country fairs, and in the little shops of remote towns almost as certainly as the *Pilgrim's Progress* and *Robinson Crusoe.* (Reed, 5)

A comparison of Gessner with Bunyan and Defoe indicates the breadth of his appeal and popularity. The statement that the *Death of Abel* was "printed at country presses" also indicates that there must be many editions that are not known, since all the known English editions were printed at London, Boston, or Philadelphia.

I have given examples of Gessner's prose style in the original and in Mrs. Collyer's translation. In discussing this style the *Quarterly Review* goes so far as to suggest that *"The Death of Abel"* was probably one of the models upon which Macpherson formed his Ossianic style." (Reed, 52) Gessner's style is basically an attempt to write poetry without the use of artificial expression; and in addition to the suggestion of a stylistic influence on James Macpherson, it should be noted that Gessner's poetry displays in many ways the natural usage of language recommended so strongly by Wordsworth in his "Preface to the Lyrical Ballads."

No other German writer before the time of Goethe and Schiller so excited the poetic imagination of English poets as did Gessner. He was one of the first German writers to be read and discussed by all of the major English poets of the late eighteenth century, and many of them read his works in the original German as well as in English translation. For at least one English poet, Byron, Gessner's *Der Tod Abels* was one of the texts from which he learned German. And to Gessner goes the distinction of having been one of the German writers whose influence in English Romantic poetry was considered to be of such significance that a book has been written on the subject. It is beyond the scope of this survey to attempt to amplify or expand the work of Bertha Reed concerning Gessner's influence on English literature. As a summation, however, two prominent ideas of Gessner's should be brought into focus. One is his critical concept of art as an expression of nature rather than an imitation of nature. The other is his attitude toward nature and particularly his sensitive feeling for animal life.

The attitude toward nature in the eighteenth century was complex indeed,[8] but the primary critical attitude during most of the century was that art should be an imitation of nature. The concept of art as expressive rather than as imitative was certainly one concept that contributed greatly to the new literature that appeared toward the end of the century and on into the nineteenth century.[9] Salomon Gessner was one of the first literary critics of great popularity to emphasize this distinction, and the fact that Gessner was a gifted landscape painter as well as poet enabled him to see and express these ideas most clearly.

His concept of art as expression rather than as imitation was stated first in England in his *Letters on Landscape Painting* (1776) which was a translation of *Briefe über die Landschaftsmahlerey* (1772).[10] In this essay Gessner discusses what he considers the relationship between landscape painting and poetry, both of which arts he practiced successfully, and in so doing he reveals a great deal about his attitude toward nature poetry and the difference between his poetry and that of Brockes and Thomson.

> My natural inclination led me to landscapes; I sought with ardour the means of satisfying my desire, and embarrassed in the route I should take, I said to myself, there is but one model, there is but one master; and I determined to draw after nature. But I soon found, that this great and sublime master does not explain himself clearly but to those that have learnt to comprehend him. My precision in following him every where led me astray. I lost myself in those minute details that destroy the effect of the whole. I had not catch'd that manner which without being servile or slight, expresses the true character of objects.... In a word, my eye confined too closely to one point, was not accustomed to embrace a large extent. (90)

This is a principle that applied equally well to literary theory and is reminiscent of a statement of Lessing in his sixteenth *Literaturbrief* (1759).

> Die Güte eines Werkes beruhet nicht auf einzeln Schönheiten; diese einzelne Schönheiten müssen ein schönes Ganze ausmachen, oder der Kenner kann sie nicht anders, als mit einem zürnenden Missvergnügen lesen. Nur wenn das Ganze untadelhaft befunden wird, muß der Kunstrichter von einer nachtheiligen Zergliederung abstehen, und das Werk so, wie der Philosoph die Welt, betrachten.

Gessner was probably not aware when he recommended expression of Nature in preference to imitation of nature that he was saying anything Thomson or Brockes had not said, and this is why Gessner's poetry is as much a climax of the past as a new beginning. Gessner

felt he was following in the footsteps of Thomson and Brockes, as he truly was, but without realizing it he was also suggesting innovations. His reliance on the past is evident from his praise of Thomson and Brockes as painters of nature.

> How I pity the unfeeling landscape painter, whom the sublime pictures of Tomson [sic] cannot inspire! In reading the descriptions of that great master, we seem to see the paintings of our most famous artists .... Give me leave on this occasion to revive the remembrance of one of our poets, almost forgotten; Brockes, who followed nature even in her least details, was endowed with lively and delicate sensations, felt the most gentle impressions, and was moved by the most trivial circumstances. A plant cover'd with dew and illumin'd by a bright ray of the sun roused his enthusiasm. A bird complaining for the loss of her young ones fill'd him with emotion. (102-3)

Nevertheless, the key to his new attitude toward art is the change from imitative to expressive art.

> Thus passing from various imitations to continual reflections, and then returning to nature, I found at last that my efforts became less laborious. The principal masses and forms lay'd themselves open to my sight. Effects that I had not perceiv'd struck me. I was at last able to express, by a single stroke what art cou'd not detail without prejudice. My manner became expressive. (94)

After an expansion of this principle Gessner relates these ideas to poetry.

> But since I have digressed from the practice of the art to theoretic ideas, and have indicated the means of improving the imagination, and elevating the genius, I must here recommend to the young artists the reading of good poets. What can be of more use in refining their taste, exalting their ideas, and enriching their imagination? The poet and the painter, friends and rivals, draw from the same source; they both borrow from nature and communicate their riches by rules that are analogous. (101)

In addition to his ideas on art as an expression of nature, Gessner greatly excited the Romantic mind with his concept of an animated nature that was aware of man's presence just as man was aware of the presence of nature, and although not as well formulated as Wordsworth's later ideas, Gessner's notion was something quite different from the attitudes of his precursors, Brockes and Thomson.

An example of Gessner's attitude is well displayed in the idyll "Amyntas." Amyntas the humble woodcutter and shepherd is returning to his cottage with the results of his day's labor: a few beech poles. In a cool grove he spies a young oak tree whose roots have been exposed by the stream, "und der Baum stund da, traurig und drohte zu sinken. Schade! sprach er, solltest du Baum in dies wilde Wasser stürzen; nein, dein Wipfel soll nicht zum Spiel seiner Wellen hingeworfen seyn."[11] Anne Penny's verse translation of this passage reads:

> Alas! he cried, 'tis pity thou should'st dye,
> Ere yet thy leaves maturer beauties shed,
> Or ere thy acorns spread this verdant bed;
> Forbid it Fate—this hand shall fence thee round,
> These beechen poles shall guard thy ravag'd ground.

Amytas then prepared a dam with his beech poles and tenderly replaced the soil around the roots of the young oak. Having saved the tree he prepared to return again to the forest to replace the beech poles he had used for the benefit of the oak, "aber die Dryas (die Dryaden waren Schuz-Göttinnen der Eichen) rief ihm mit lieblicher Stimme aus der Eiche zu: Sollt' ich unbelohnet dich weglassen? gütiger Hirt! sage mirs, was wünschest du zur Belohnung." Again, Anne Penny has expanded this more than slightly.

> When lo a voice of soft inchanting sound
> Issues he knows not whence, from tree or ground,
> And calls "Amyntas"—he astonish'd stands,
> His hatchet falling from his trembling hands;
> When thus the Syren Dryad of the oak
> (For such She was) in softest accents spoke:
> Young shepherd, gentlest of the rustic train,
> With whom compassion never pleads in vain;
> Say, what return my willing hand shall pay
> For thy benevolence bestow'd to day

Gessner writes as if communion with nature were a natural occurrence, and Amyntas answers the Dryad's question "was wünschest du zur Belohnung" in a most matter-of-fact manner: "O! wenn du mir zu bitten vergönnest, Nymphe! so sprach der arme Hirt; mein Nachbar Palemon ist seit der Erndte schon krank, laß ihn gesund werden! So bat der Redliche, und Palemon ward gesund." The idyll concludes with man and nature in complete harmony, and this harmony is expanded through the blessing of the Gods. "Aber Amyntas sah den mächtigen Segen in seiner Heerde und bey seinen Bäumen und Früchten, und ward ein reicher Hirt; denn die Götter lassen die Redlichen nicht ungesegnet."

The compassion for nature is in the spirit of Brockes' poetry, but the gratitude for this compassion on the part of a nature personified is something quite foreign to the empirical and rationalistic age for which Brockes is writing. It is, however, a movement toward the mysterious atmosphere of tutelary spirits, and the mood evoked by Gessner in his idylls combined with his humanitarian attitude toward animal life in *The Death of Abel* is strongly suggestive of the mood of Schiller's "Alpenjäger," Bürger's "Der wilde Jäger," Wordsworth's "Hart-Leap Well," Coleridge's "Ancient Mariner," and Burns' "To a Mouse."

One of Gessner's most poignant scenes depicting the relationship between man and animal centers around a bird. The scene is from

The Death of Abel. Adam and Eve have their first real intimation of death when they encounter a fallen bird. The horror and perplexity that overcome them on this occasion greatly intensify the tragic mood foreshadowing the impending death of their son Abel. Adam is narrating for his children the events of the first day after being driven from Eden.

> We were going on when we saw just above our heads a bird fly with feeble wing; its feathers were rough and disorder'd: it cast forth plaintive cries, and having flutter'd a little in the air, sunk down without strength among the bushes. Eve went to seek it, and beheld another lie without motion on the grass, which that we had before seen seem'd to lament. My spouse stooping over it, examin'd it with great attention, and in vain try'd to rouse it from what she believ'd to be sleep. It will not wake, she said to me, in a fearful voice, laying the bird from her trembling hand, — it will not wake. — It will never wake more! She then burst into tears, and speaking to the lifeless bird, said, Alas! the poor bird who pierc'd my ears with his cries, was perhaps thy mate. It is me! — It is me! Unhappy that I am who have brought misery and grief on every creature! For my sin these pretty harmless animals are punished. Her tears redoubled. What an event! said she, turning to me. How stiff and cold it is! It has neither voice nor motion. Its joints no longer bend. Its limbs refuse their office. Speak, Adam, is this death? Ah it is. — How I tremble! An icy cold runs thro' my bones. If the death with which we are threaten'd is like this, how terrible! (53)

Eve then compares the fate of the dead bird and its grieving mate with the terrible probablity of her separation from Adam through death.

Coleridge has written a charming poem on this theme called "The Death of the Starling."

> Pity! mourn in plaintive tone
> The lovely starling dead and gone!
> Pity mourns in plaintive tone
> The lovely starling dead and gone.
> Weep, ye Loves! and Venus! weep
> The lovely starling fall'n asleep!
> Venus sees with tearful eyes —
> In her lap the starling lies!
> While the Loves all in a ring
> Softly stroke the stiffen'd wing.

Burns, who was very sensitive to nature, has seen this relationship of man and animal exhibited through their common fate.

> I'm truly sorry man's dominion
> Has broken Nature's social union,
> An' justifies that ill opinion
>   Which makes thee startle
> At me, thy poor earth born companion,
>   An fellow mortal!

Wordsworth, in "Hart-Leap Well" describes the desolate condition of the area where a noble stag was slain. The young shepherd in relating the story of the event says:

Some say that here a murder has been done
And blood cries out for blood.

Gessner links the fate of a bird with the fate of Adam and Eve, and suggests the impending death of their son at the hands of his brother. Burns calls a mouse his "fellow mortal," and Wordsworth suggests that the death of a stag was actually a murder. With this feeling of brotherhood between man and animal, it is not unlikely that Coleridge was suggesting in the murder of the albatross a crime as terrible as the fratricide committed by Cain; followed by the curse of wandering.

Gessner's portrayal of the first fratricide together with the brooding, melancholy character of Cain had a peculiar fascination for the English Romantics; Byron and Coleridge each wrote a *Cain*. Byron first read Gessner's *Death of Abel* when he was eight years old, and when he began to study German, he tells us:

> Abel was one of the first books my German master read to me; and whilst he was crying his eyes out over its pages, I thought that any other than Cain had hardly committed a crime in ridding the world of so dull a fellow as Gessner made brother Abel. I always thought Cain a fine subject, and when I took it up, I determined to treat it strictly after the Mosaic account. (Reed, 97)

Coleridge was also fascinated with Gessner's characterization of Cain. In 1798 he suggested to Wordsworth that they jointly compose a sequel to Gessner's *Death of Abel*, to be known as *The Wanderings of Cain*. In the preface to this work Coleridge writes:

> The title and subject were suggested by myself, who likewise drew out the scheme and the contents for each of the three books or cantos, of which the work was to consist, and which, the reader is to be informed, was to have been finished in one night! My partner undertook the first canto: I the second: and whichever had *done first*, was to set about the third.... Methinks I see his grand and noble countenance as at the moment when having despatched my own portion of the task at full fingerspeed, I hastened to him with my manuscript—that look of humorous despondency fixed on his almost blank sheet of paper, and then its silent mock-piteous admission of failure struggling with the sense of the exceeding ridiculousness of the whole scheme—which broke up in a laugh: and the *Ancient Mariner* was written instead.

This last statement by Coleridge has often been underestimated. His mind was struggling with the poetic resolution to the problem of fratricide, curse, wandering, and penance, "and the *Ancient Mariner* was written instead."

Salomon Gessner was constantly used as a source of ideas by Coleridge. A striking example is Coleridge's poem, "The Picture, or the Lover's Resolution," which is actually a translation and expansion of Gessner's idyll "Der feste Vorsatz." Coleridge has expanded Gessner's forty-five lines of prose into 186 lines of verse. By eliminating the lines added by Coleridge, the translation becomes obvious.

Wohin irret mein verwundeter Fuß, durch Dornen und dichtverwebte Sträuche?...

Die rötlichen Stämme der Fichten und die schlanken Stämme der Eichen steigen wildem Gebüsche hervor und tragen ein trauriges Gewölb' über mir; ... Hier will ich mich hinsetzen, an den hohlen, vormoderten Eichstamm, den ein Netz von Efeu umwickelt; hier will ich mich hinsetzen, wo kein menschlicher Fußtritt noch hingedrungen ist, wo niemand mich find't, ...

Through weeds and thorns, and matted underwood
I force my way ...
                    With dun-red bark
The fir-trees, and the unfrequent slender oak,
Forth from this tangle wild of bush and brake
Soar up, and form a melancholy vault
High o'er me, murmuring like a distant sea ...
Here will I seat myself, beside this old,
Hollow, and weedy oak, which ivy-twine
Clothes as with net-work: here will I couch my limbs,
Close by this river, in this silent shade,
As safe and sacred from the step of man
As an invisible world—unheard, unseen, ...

Gessner is not remembered as one of the great German critics or even as one of the great German poets, and many of the works that were translated into English in this Pre-romantic period are now in the realms of forgotten literature. It is often such minor works of literature, however, that prepare the way for a great "flowering" period in which works of universal and lasting value are produced. Likewise, it does happen that a poet such as Gessner, adhering to literary concepts from a previous generation, can have insights and critical judgments that are somehow new and appealing, and that greatly stimulate the new generation of poets. Lessing had delineated the difference between art and poetry, but Gessner was able to talk about the expressive nature of both art and poetry in a way that was in advance of many of Lessing's ideas. So too, Gessner could discuss the advantage to be derived from reading Thomson and Brockes, but in his own poetry he made innovations not considered by either of his precursors. Gessner's poetry was one of the forces that found literature at a moment of indecision and hurried it on to a new climax.

VII. CONCLUSION

In the "Introduction" to this study we examined the history of the idea that there were no German literary influences in England from the time of the Thirty Year's War until the late eighteenth century. As I stated there, many of the scholars who arrived at this conclusion were competent and highly esteemed in their field, and we cannot assume that their critical consensus was reached hastily or irresponsibly. Nevertheless, the facts presented in this study indicate that this critical consensus is not valid. In the case of German-English literary relations scholars have reasoned: "Since German literary and cultural life was paralyzed by the Thirty Year's War and went through a slow century-long recovery, there could not possibly have been any cultural stimulation from that country until the time of Klopstock, Lessing, Wieland, and their successors, and therefore the tedious task of detailed investigation is unnecessary." This purely intellectual, logical approach to comparative literature was bound to result in failure. English indifference to German literature was both asserted categorically and demonstrated by these supposed conditions. The logical or theoretical approach to literary scholarship may in some cases be enlightening, provided the basic assumption or premise is correct. In this instance it was not, but the myth about the destructiveness of the Thirty Year's War lives on.

As I also suggested in the introduction, we must replace this method of *a priori* assumptions and exclusions with a method of *a posteriori* conclusions from phenomena observed in context. If we first look at what is there, note the relations, and only then decide whether they have literary relevance or not, we obtain remarkably different results. Naturally, a survey of the whole course of German-English scientific relations at this time will for the most part be of small or no literary relevance. But here and there, where we might least expect it, something of true and even central literary significance can turn up. That is even more the case in the field of music: the Handel-Pope relationship, for example, and the associations of Johann Christian Pepusch and Johann Friedrich Lampe with John Gay and Henry Carey clearly had literary implications. Even more important as well as more subtle and difficult to trace are the effects the new music had on the development of English lyric poetry during its pre-Romantic and Romantic phases. In the field of art and art criticism we find clear literary relations, and the question of the Winckelmann influence in the new Hellenism to appear in English Romantic poetry has never been fully answered. Most of all, these considerations apply to the new wave of religious individualism and subjectivity, largely German inspired, that swept over England. How this could be kept separate from the new wave of lyric individualism and subjectivity in English poetry it would be difficult even for the champions of literary isolation to explain. The attempt to divorce literature from religion has resulted in the neglect of even the purely literary activity of German theologians in England. Johann Arndt's *True Christianity* is a devotional work and also a literary masterpiece. Many of the volumes of hymns translated into English were not only great lyric poems in the original, they also found able translators and English poets who followed their inspiration. Charles Wesley and William Cowper attest to the power and influence of German hymnody, and I have cited the example of Shelley's affinity to the German hymn and Coleridge's expression of gratitude to the German mystics to show how this stimulus extended deep into the Romantic period. These German and English hymns gave life and emotional vitality to the religious movement known as the Great Awakening and probably accounted to a large extent for its widespread and long-lasting success. The emotional atmosphere and general cultural effect of this Great Awakening, in turn, prepared the way for the reception of the next large body of German literary works, those with Biblical themes and highly sensitive, subjective, emotional treatment. Specifically: Klopstock's *Messiah* and his *Death of Adam*, Wieland's *Trial of Abraham*, Bodmer's *Noah*, and the most popular and important of all, Gessner's *Death of Abel*. These, again, less in theme than in treatment, led over to the subjective sensibility that came to characterize the new poetic work of the pre-Romantic and Romantic writers. One indication of their continuing exemplary position is the popularity of Klopstock's *Messiah* and Gessner's *Death of Abel* well into the nineteenth century. Indeed one critic of the Romantic period evaluated the popularity of *The Death of Abel* by placing it in the exclusive class occupied by Bunyan's *Pilgrim's Progress* and Defoe's *Robinson Crusoe*.

As a "first survey" attempting to cover a very broad area I have not followed many a lead that may well prove important in German-English literary relations, such as: the possible literary associations of

Locke and Addison during their stay in Germany (I know of one contribution that Addison's stay in Germany made to the *Spectator*); the English relations of Johann Mattheson, musician, editor, and secretary to the English ambassador in Hamburg and to the German ambassador in London; Defoe's German motifs, not only in *Robinson Crusoe* but also in his *Memoirs of a Cavalier* and *The Fortunate Mistress*; the elusive English translation of David Fassmann's *Gespräche aus dem Reiche derer Todten* and its connections with Elizabeth Rowe's *Letters from the Dead* dedicated to Edward Young; the short popularity of *The High German Doctor*; the early eighteenth-century English periodicals (George Baker examined only five periodicals and reported that they were "replete with notices and reviews of books published in Germany," but he failed to understand the possible literary relevance of these notices); Gottsched's claim (neither challenged nor substantiated to my knowledge) that Swift received the idea for his *Tale of a Tub* from Martin Rinkart's *Eislebischen christlichen Ritter*; and the complete story of Jacob Boehme's "purely" literary influences in England, such as his influence on Henry Brooke's *Fool of Quality*. The literary significance of two important critical works translated into English has never been fully investigated: Georg Friedrich Meier's *The Merry Philosopher; or, Thoughts on Jesting Containing Rules . . . and the Criterion for Distinguishing True and Genuine Wit*, (London, 1764), and Justus Möser's *Harlequin; or, a Defence of the Grotesque-Comic Performances*, (London, 1766). There were also works on art criticism and works on music criticism published in England in the early and mid eighteenth century that need to be more carefully examined for their relations to literary criticism.

My study has been an exploratory topographical survey of a period when German literary and cultural influences in England were said to have been non-existent. Enough evidence, however, has been assembled to indicate that the literary and general cultural stimuli from Germany in the early eighteenth century were not only constant and plentiful, they were also significant for certain developments and changes in English literature. What are now needed are more intensive and extensive studies in this wide field. With the irrelevant factors, *a priori* assumptions, meaningless clichés, and unwarranted exclusions that beclouded the issues safely cleared out of the way, the scholar can now proceed on a higher level of research. Our task will be an easier one and the results more meaningful.

NOTES

CHAPTER I:

¹ Gilbert Waterhouse, *Literary Relations of England and Germany in the* 17th *Century*, (Cambridge, 1914).
² Rufus M. Jones, *Spiritual Reformers in the* 16th *and* 17th *Centuries*, (Boston, 1914), and Margaret L. Bailey, *Milton and Jacob Boehme*, (New York, 1914).
³ Caroline Spurgeon, *Mysticism in English Literature*, (Cambridge, 1913).
⁴ Joseph Walter, *Über den Einfluß des* 30-*jährigen Krieges auf die deutsche Sprache und Literatur*, (Prag-Kleinseite, 1871).
⁵ "Daß im 17. Jahrhundert die Werke Jacob Boehmes übersetzt und in England verbreitet wurden, ist wohl bekannt, doch geschah dies natürlich aus theologischem, nicht aus literarischem Interesse." Georg Herzfeld, "Zur Geschichte der deutschen Literatur in England," *Archiv für das Studium der neueren Sprachen* (CV, 1900). [translation mine]
⁶ Thomas George Tucker, *The Foreign Debt of English Literature*, (London, 1907), 238.
⁷ "Bis gegen Ende des vorigen Jahrhunderts waren die deutsche Sprache und Literatur in England gar nicht oder nur wenig beachtet." Otto Weddigen, "Die Vermittler deutschen Geistes in England und Nordamerika," *Archiv für das Studium der neueren Sprachen*, LIX (1878), 131. [translation mine]
⁸ Leslie Stephen, "The Importation of German," *Studies of a Biographer* (New York, 1904), 42.
⁹ Thomas Babington Macaulay, *The Works of Lord Macaulay Complete*, edited by his sister Lady Trevelyan, in eight volumes (London, 1871), VII, 65.
¹⁰ "Mit Zins und Zinsenzins konnte jetzt die deutsche Literatur das Kapital zurückerstatten, das sie nicht nur in früheren Perioden, da sie in unselbständiger Nachahmung ein kümmerliches Dasein gefristet, sondern auch jetzt wieder im Beginn ihrer höchsten von England entliehen hatte." Ernst Margraf, *Einfluß der deutschen Literatur auf die englische am Ende des achtzehnten Jahrhunderts und im ersten Drittel des neunzehnten Jahrhuhderts* (Leipzig, 1901), 6. [translation mine]
¹¹ Tucker, 231.
¹² *Ibid.*, 238.
¹³ "Im 17. Jahrhundert konnten die Engländer in dem von dem dreißigjährigen Krieg verwüsteten Deutschland keine literarische Anregung finden." E. Koeppel, *Deutsche Strömungen in der englischen Litteratur* (Straßburg, 1910), 7. [translation mine]
¹⁴ Laurie Magnus, *English Literature in its Foreign Relations* 1300-1800 (London & New York, 1927), 181.
¹⁵ "Ich muß aber zu meinem Bedauern gestehen, daß in diesem Kapitel nicht nur mancher einzelne hervorragende Deutsche, sondern ganze Klassen solcher fehlen . . .
In folge meiner Abwesenheit von England war es mir nicht möglich in diesem Kapitel

den Plan zu verfolgen, nach welchem ich die ersten fünf Kapitel ausgeführt, nämlich nicht nur biographische Skizzen von einzelnen Deutschen zu geben, sondern auch ein Bild der Beziehungen zwischen England und Deutschland zu entwerfen und den Einfluß anzudeuten, den unsere Landsleute in England auf diese Beziehungen ausgeübt." Karl Heinrich Schaible, *Geschichte der Deutschen in England* (Straßburg, 1885). [translation mine]

[16] G. H. Turnbull, *Hartlib, Dury, and Comenius* (London, 1947).

[17] James Taft Hatfield, "John Wesley's Translation of German Hymns," *PMLA*, XI (1896), 171-199, and Henry Bett, *The Hymns of Methodism*, (London, 1956).

[18] Harold Jantz, "German Baroque Literature," *Modern Language Notes*, LVII (1962), pp. 337-367.

CHAPTER II:

[1] John Julian, *Dictionary of Hymnology* (London, 1892), 412.

[2] Clifford W. Towlson, *Moravian and Methodist* (London, 1957), 203.

[3] *Anton Wilhelm Böhmens ... Sämtliche Erbauliche Schriften* ... mit einer Vorrede von dem Leben des Verfassers begleitet von Johann Jacob Rambach, (Altona, 1731), p. 42. The *Vorrede* was translated into English as: *Memoirs of the Life and Death of the late Reverend Mr. Anthony William Boehm*, (London, 1735), by Johann Christian Jacobi.

[4] *Ibid.*, and again in the *Memoirs*, p. 40. See note 3.

[5] *Memoirs.* See note 3.

[6] Sir George Grove, *Grove's Dictionary of Music and Musicians*, 9th ed., edited by Eric Blom (New York, 1959), IV, 431. Article signed W. S. Rockstro and Walter H. Frere.

[7] Samuel Willoughby Duffield, *English Hymns: Their Authors and History* (New York and London, 1886), 90.

[8] John Christian Jacobi, *Psalmodia Germanica*, (London, 1722), unnumbered page ix.

[9] *Ibid.*

[10] Henry Bett, in *The Hymns of Methodism* (London, 1956), 33, discusses Wesley's use of the word "Herrnhuth" in this hymn.

[11] Thomas Herbert, *John Wesley as Editor and Author* (Princeton, 1940), 49.

[12] Not August Hermann Francke as Towlson says, but his son, Gotthelf August Francke. The father had died in 1727.

[13] Hatfield, 180-181. The most complete list of German hymns translated by Wesley is in Henry Bett, *The Hymns of Methodism*, p. 30 ff.

[14] In addition to Bett, Herbert, and Towlson, op. cit., Thomas Boswell Shepherd, *Methodism and the Literature of the Eighteenth Century* (London, 1940), Jeremiah Bascom Reeves, *The Hymn as Literature* (New York and London, 1924), and F. B. Harvey, "Methodism and the Romantic Movement," *London Quarterly* (July, 1934), 289-302 are of some interest; however, a full treatment of the religious atmosphere in English Romanticism has not been undertaken.

[15] It should be noted that Shelley was one of the more able translators of German. His translation of the "Prologue in Heaven" from Goethe's *Faust* remains one of the few examples that the *Faust* can be translated provided the translator is a poet of the same stature as Goethe. It is unfortunate that Shelley did not translate the entire drama.

[16] The reason an interpreter was needed was that the Latin spoken on the continent was pronounced differently from the Latin spoken in England.

[17] The role of Zinzendorf in the controversy is discussed in Chapter III. It is interesting to note that after over 225 years the Methodists have now concluded a merger with their old comrades, the Moravians.

[18] Martin Madan, William Cowper's cousin and a convert of John Wesley.

[19] Louis I. Bredvold, editor, *Eighteenth Century Poetry & Prose*, (New York, 1956), p. 882.

CHAPTER III:

1 Henry Eyster Jacobs, *A History of the Evangelical Lutheran Church in the United States* (New York, 1893), 143.
2 *Anton Wilhelm Böhmens . . . Erbauliche Briefe* (Altona and Flensburg, 1737), letter dated September, 1714, to a "Hrn. N.N.".
3 Quoted from *Dictionary of National Biography*, article: "Anthony Horneck," by Leslie Stephen.
4 Towlson, p. 17.
5 *The Happy Ascetick: or, the best Exercise . . .* (1681); *The Fire of the Altar: or, Certain Directions how to raise the Soul into Holy Flames before,at, and after the receiving the blessed sacrament of the Lord's Supper . . .*, (1684), (13th ed. 1718); *The First Fruits of Reason* (1686); *A Phisicotheological Discourse on the Divine Being . . . and the Danger of Enthusiasm* (1698) (written with John Turner); *A Votive Ode for the Happy Delivery of . . . the Princess of Wales.*
6 The best treatment of this period in Wesley's life is: Vivian Hubert Howard Green, *The Young Mr. Wesley* (London, 1961).
7 Boehm's works and letters were published at Altona by Johann Jacob Rambach in three volumes under the title: *Sämtliche Erbauliche Schriften*, Volume I, 1731, Volume II, 1732, Volume III, part 1, 1733 and Volume III, part 2 (*Erbauliche Briefe*) 1737. See Chapter II, note 3.
8 For a thorough treatment of these emigrants see: Walter Allen Knittle, *Early Eighteenth Century Palatine Emigration*, (Philadelphia, 1937).
9 Anton Wilhelm Boehm, *Das verlangte, nicht erlangte Canaan bey den Lust-Gräbern, oder ausführliche Beschreibung von der unglücklichen Reise derer jüngsthin aus Teutschland nach dem Engelländischen in Amerika gelegenen Carolina und Pensylvanien wallenden Pilgrim* (Franckfurt u. Leipzig, 1711).
10 Karl Heinrich Schaible, *Geschichte der Deutschen in England von den ersten germanischen Ansiedlungen in Britannien bis zum Ende des 18. Jahrhunderts* (Straßburg, 1855), 342.
11 For Law's library see: *A Catalogue of the Library at King's Cliffe Northamptonshire* (King's Cliffe, 1927).
12 All quotations are from: John Arndt, *True Christianity, . . . Originally translated into English by Rev. A. W. Boehm, German Chaplain at the Court of St. James, and Published in London, A.D. 1712 . . . A New American edition . . .* (Philadelphia, 1872).
13 See the Bibliography for a list of the significant works in the area.
14 *A Catalogue of the Library of the late John Byrom*, (London, 1848).
15 Samuel Taylor Coleridge, *Biographia Literaria*, (London, 1960), "Everyman's Library" edition, Chapter IX, pp. 80, 86-87.
16 *Allgemeine Deutsche Biographie*, Article on Zinzendorf by P. Tschackert.
17 Coleridge, Chapter IX, p. 83.

CHAPTER IV:

1 George Sherburn, "The Restoration and Eighteenth Century," *A Literary History of England*, ed. Albert C. Baugh, (New York, 1948), p. 832.
2 George M. Baker, "Some References to German Literature in English Magazines of the Early Eighteenth Century," *MLN* XXIV (1909), 112.
3 Anna Alice Chapin, *Masters of Music*, (New York, 1933), 46.
4 Elbert Hubbard, *Georg Friedrich Händel*, (East Aurora, N.Y., 1901), 68.
5 Ibid., 71.
6 Johann Elias Schlegel, "Aesthetische und dramaturgische Schriften," *Deutsche Litteraturdenkmale des 18. und 19. Jahrhunderts*, XXVI, ed. Johann von Antoniewicz (Heilbronn, 1887), 223, 224.
7 The entire *Preface* shows remarkable similarities of thought to the critical ideas of Johann Elias Schlegel and Lessing's sixteenth and seventeenth *Literaturbriefe*, (1759).
8 Most of the material on this subject was written from the aesthetic viewpoint, and not

the critical. Cf. Abbé du Bos, *Critical Reflections on Poetry, Painting, and Music*, Tr. Thomas Nugent, (London, 1748); James Beattie, *Essays on Poetry and Music* (London, 1776); John Brown, *A Dissertation on ... Poetry and Music* (London, 1763); Johann Georg Sulzer, "Ausdruck in der Musik," *Allgemeine Theorie der schönen Künste* (Leibzig, 1771-74). Important suggestions are also found in Harold Jantz' article, "German Baroque Literature," *MLN* LVII (1962), 363 ff. The first thorough treatment is M. Gloria Flaherty's *In Defense of the Opera: a Survey of German Critical Writings on Opera from 1678 to 1770*, Diss., Johns Hopkins University, 1965.

⁹ Michael Kitson writes of this portrait: "As a work of art this was perhaps an inspired accident, untypical of Kneller and not quite sustained by the technical skill necessary to carry it off. Nevertheless, it is one of the most original portraits of its time. Together with certain portrait-busts by Coysevox, it brings into focus the 'new man' of the 18th century: the intellectual-rationalist in spirit, sceptical, urbane and cosmopolitan." *The Age of Baroque* (New York, McGraw Hill, 1966), 59. The portrait is reproduced there, illustration ≠ 32.

¹⁰ Thomas Carlyle, *History of Freidrich II of Prussia* (London, 1898), VI, 255.

¹¹ Bayard Q. Morgan, *A Critical Bibliography of German Literature in English Translation* (New York and London, 1965), lists only one translation prior to 1770, that of Winckelmann's *Gedanken über die Nachahmung der griechischen Werke*, but lists it under two different titles, the other being: *Gedanken über die Malerei und Bildhauerkunst der Griechen*. See Morgan, 10277 and 10278.

¹² Hans Füssli, a cousin to Heinrich. This discovery was made by a graduate student at the University of Colorado who is now undertaking a thorough study of the London-Zürich art circles.

¹³ *Itinera Alpina*, translated into German by the Zürich critic Johann Georg Sulzer.

CHAPTER V:

¹ George M. Baker, 113.
² *Ibid.*
³ Fritz Schmidt, *Tabellen der deutschen Literatur* (Bonn, 1950), 172.
⁴ Harold Jantz, "Brockes' Poetic Apprenticeship," *MLN* LVII (1962), 440.
⁵ Thomas Newton, *The Works of the Right Reverend Thomas Newton*, 3 Vols. (London, 1782) I, 47.
⁶ Bertha Reed Coffman, "The Influence of English Literature on Friedrich von Hagedorn," *Modern Philogy* XII (1914), 121 and 179 ff., and XIII (1915).
⁷ For a first examination of this "Vorrede" see: Harold Jantz, "German Baroque Literature," *MLN* LVII (1962) 365ff.
⁸ Quotations from Friedrich von Hagedorn, "Versuch einiger Gedichte," *Deutsche Literaturdenkmale des 18. Jahrhunderts*, X, Hrsg. Bernhard Seuffert (Heilbron, 1883).
⁹ Thomas Lediard, *The German Spy*, 2nd ed. (London, 1740), 292-93. The work on "representations" is: Thomas Lediard, *Eine Collection Curieuser Vorstellungen in Illuminationen* (Hamburg, 1730).

CHAPTER VI:

¹ From Hamann's discussion of the Scheffler hymn in "Betrachtungen zu Kirchenliedern," *Tagebuch eines Christen*, Volume I of *Sämtliche Werke* (Wien, 1949).
² Henry Betts makes the attempt to distinguish John Wesley's hymns from those of his brother Charles in *The Hymns of Methodism*, Chapter III, "John Wesley or Charles Wesley?".
³ Josef Nadler, *Johann Georg Hamann* (Salzburg, 1949), 76.
⁴ The epithet "The German Stories" was evidently attached to this type of German literature by the English writer of Gothic novels, Clara Reeve. See J. M. S. Tompkins, *The Popular Novel in England* 1770-1800 (London, 1932), 67.

[5] Morgan lists only one edition in his *Bibliography*, but the copy I have before me is the "second edition," (London, 1762).

[6] See Bayard Q. Morgan and A. R. Hohlfeld, *German Literature in British Magazines 1750-1860* (Madison, 1949).

[7] For an account of the reviews of Gessner's works in England see Bertha Reed, *The Influence of Solomon Gessner upon English Literature* (Philadelphia, 1905).

[8] For an attempt at organizing this complexity see Arthur O. Lovejoy, "Nature as Aesthetic Norm," *MLN* XLII (1927), 444-450. Reprinted in *Essays in the History of Ideas* (Baltimore, 1948).

[9] Still the most comprehensive treatment of this broad area is given by Meyer H. Abrams, *The Mirror and the Lamp* (New York, 1953). The scope of this excellent book, however, does not permit a treatment of many of the individual aspects of this concept of imitation and expression in literature.

[10] The edition from which I quote is: *New Idylles by Gessner Translated by W. Hooper MD. With a Letter to M. Fuslin, on Landscape Painting, ...* (London, 1776).

[11] Quotations in German from Salomon Gessner, *Schriften*, vter Theil, (Zürich, 1772), "Amyntas" beginning on p. 239.

SUPPLEMENT

A CHRONOLOGICAL BIBLIOGRAPHY OF GERMAN LITERATURE
IN ENGLISH TRANSLATION 1700-1770

The importance of this bibliography is primarily for historical studies, and for this reason the chronological arrangement was considered more useful than an alphabetical arrangement. The major sources for titles have been the British Museum *Catalogue*, the Library of Congress *Catalogue*, Bayard Q. Morgan's *Bibliography of German Literature in English Translation*, Charles Evans' *American Bibliography*, John Julian's *Dictionary of Hymnology*, and William Gunn Malin's *Catalogue of Books Relating to . . . the History of the Unitas Fratrum*, plus several sources of lesser importance. [See the "Bibliography of Works Relating to this Study"] The result is the most complete listing of German literature in English translation for this period. It will be noted occasionally that a later edition of a work is listed without mentioning the earlier editions. In this case a reference to the earlier edition has not been located. This bibliography contains primarily translations published separately. Morgan and Hohlfeld, *German Literature in British Magazines* 1750-1860 (Madison, 1949) lists translations appearing in periodicals, but only for the period from 1750. There is no bibliography of translations appearing in periodicals for the period 1700-1750.

1700
Comenius, Johann Amos. Sensualium pictus, or a picture and nomenclature of all the chief things that are in the world . . . written by the author in Latin and High Dutch and translated into English by Charles Hoole, M. A. Printed for J. Sprint at the Bell in Little Britain.

The famous and delightful history of Fortunatus and his two sons. 7th edition. Printed by and for T. Norris at the Looking Glass on London Bridge. [date?]

The History of the damnable life and deserved death of Doctor John Faustus. C. Brown for M. Hotham. London. [date?]

The History of Reynard the Fox, and Renardine his son. In two parts. With morals to each chapter, explaining what appears doubtful or allegorical: and every chapter illustrated with a curious devise or picture. Written by an eminent statesman of the German Empire, and since done into English. Printed by the booksellers of London and Westminister. [date?]

The History of the wicked life and miserable end of Dr. J. Faustus. Translated from the original copy printed at Frankford. For J. Back. London. [date?]

1701
The most delectable history of Reynard the Fox. To which may now be added a second part of the said history, as also the shifts of Reynardine the son of Reynard the Fox. 3 pt. T. Olive, for E Brewster. London.

1702

Culmann, Leonhard. Sentences for children, English and Latin. For the first entrers [sic] into Latin. Translated by Charles Hoole. Printed by B. Green, and J. Allen. Boston.

The life of Prince Eugene of Savoy. Translated [out of German] into French, and now into English. London.

Parmannus, Matthaeus Gothofredus. A treatise of salvation. Written originally in High Dutch by Parmannus. Translated from the 2nd edition. Printed for T. Newborough at the Golden Ball in St. Paul's Churchyard.

Pufendorf, Samuel. The Compleat History of Sweden, from its origin to this time. Written by the famous Samuell Puffendorf. Translated from the original High-Dutch, and carefully continued down to this present year. [by C. Brockwell]. J. Wild. London.

Pufendorf, Samuel. An Introduction to the History of the principal Kingdoms and States of Europe. 5th ed. with additions. London.

1703

Pufendorf, Samuel. Of the law of nature and nations. Eight books. Written in Latin by the Baron Pufendorf. Translated into English, from the best edition. With a short introduction. Oxford, Printed by L. Lichfield, for A. and J. Churchil. [Dedication signed by Basil Kennett, who translated part of the work; book V translated by William Percivale.]

1705

Comenius, Johann Amos. Sensualium Pictus, . . . J. A. Commenius's Visible World . . . translated . . . by Charles Hoole. For John Sprint. London.

Francke, August Hermann. Pietas Hallensis; or a public demonstration of the footsteps of a Divine Being yet in the world: in an historical narration of the Orphan House and other charitable institutions at Glaucha near Hall in Saxony . . . and now done out of High-Dutch into English. With a preface bringing it down to the present time; together with a short history of Pietism and an appendix, containing several instruments and public papers relating to this work. [translated by Anton Wilhelm Boehm] London.

Mandelslo, Johann Albrecht von. The Voyages and Travels of J. A. Mandelslo . . . into the East Indies in the years 1638, 1639, and 1640. In Harris, J. *Navigantium atque Itinerantium Biblioteca*, Vol. 2.

Pufendorf, Samuel. A Compleat History of Europe . . . taken from . . . Pufendorf. London.

Pufendorf, Samuel. An introduction to the history of Asia, Africa, and America. London.

Pufendorf, Samuel. The whole duty of man according to the law of nature. London.

1706

A Collection of curious travels. The first containing Dr. [Leonhard] Rauwolf's itinerary. Translated from the High-Dutch by Nicholas Staphorst. 2nd edition. Published by Mr. John Ray. London.

Francke, August Hermann. Manductio ad lectionem Scripturae Sacrae. Londini. [The appendix is in English.]

Francke, August Hermann. Nicodemus, or a treatise against the fear of Man. Done into English [by A. W. Boehm]. London.

Francke, August Hermann. An abstract of the marvellous Foot-steps of Divine Providence, in the building of a very large hospital . . . at Glaucha near Hall. With a preface . . . by J. Woodward. London. [Translated by A. W. Boehm].

King, John. A compleat English guide for High Germans. By J. King, Master of both languages in London. Sold by W. Freeman and B. Baker.

Pufendorf, Samuel. An introduction to the history of the principal States of Europe. 6th ed. From the original High-Dutch, with appendix never printed before containing an introduction to the history of the principal sovereign states of Italy. London.

Pufendorf, Samuel. A short account of the union between Sweden, Denmark and Norway ... Taken from Pufendorf's History of Sweden. Literature to be perus'd by Scotsmen at this juncture. [Edinburgh, 1706].

Schopperus, Hartmann. The crafty courtier, or, the fable of Reinard the fox; Newly done into English verse, from antient Latin Iambics of H[artmann] Schopperus. London.

1707

Francke, August Hermann. Pietas Hallensis. Or, an abstract of the marvellous footsteps of divine providence in the building of a very large hospital ... at Glaucha near Hall, in Saxony. 2nd enlarged ed. by Augustus Hermannus Franck and Josiah Woodward. To which is added a History of Pietism. London, printed and sold by J. Downing.

1708

Arndt, Johann. Johannis Arndtii ... de vero Christianismo libri quatuor ... cura & studio Antonii Wilhelmi Boemi. Accedit huic editioni nova praefatio de vita & scriptis Arndtianis. [With a portrait] 2 tom. J. Downing: Londini. [This important work was published in London by Boehm to prepare for the English translation which appeared in 1712 ff.]

Lyra Davidica, or a collection of divine songs and hymns, partly new composed, partly translated from the High German and Latin hymns, and set to easy and pleasant tunes. London, J. Walsh.

The most pleasing and delightful history of Reynard the fox. London. [See Morgan, A 453].

Tauler, Johann. Evangelical poverty exemplified in the life of our blessed Saviour and his Apostles. Translated from the High Dutch. London.

1709

Francke, August Hermann. Faith in Christ, inconsistent with a sollicitious concern about the things of this world. A sermon [on Matt. vi. 25-33] preach'd ... 1708 at Hall in Saxony. Now done into English [by Anton Wilhelm Boehm]. London.

Francke, August Hermann. Nicodemus. Or a treatise against the fear of man. Done into English [by Anton Wilhelm Boehm]. 2nd ed. London.

The German Rogue, or, the life and merry adventures of Till Eulenspiegel. Made English from the High-Dutch. London. [See Morgan A78]

1710

Arends, Wilhelm Erasmus. Early Piety Recommended in the Life and Death of Christlieb Leberecht von Exter. Recommended by Augustus Hermannus Franck. Render'd from the High-Dutch into English. J. Downing. London. [Date?]

Francke, August Hermann. Pietas Hallensis. Or, an abstract of the marvellous footsteps of divine providence. Part 2. London. [Translated by Anton Wilhelm Boehm]

Pufendorf, Samuel. Of the Law of Nature and of Nations. Translated into English [by Basil Kennet and others]. 2nd ed ... corrected, and compared with Mr. Barbeyrac's French translation with the addition of his notes. H. and J. Churchill. Oxford.

1711

Daut, Johann Max. The Approaching Judgments of God upon the Roman Empire, and whole false and impenitent Christendom; with the Fall of Babylon, and the Redemption of Sion. Translated out of High Dutch by B. Furly. Printed for the Booksellers of London & Westminister. London.

Erndtel, Christian Heinrich. The relation of a journey into England in the years 1706 and 1707 by a Saxon Physician in a letter to this friend at Dresden by C. H. Ed. [i.e. C. H. Erndtel]. London.

1712

Arndt, Johann. Of True Christianity. Now done into English. D. Brown and J. Downing. London. [The translator's dedicatory epistle is signed "Anthony William Boehm." Rambach,in his history of Boehm's life in England says: "Das erste Volumen kam 1712 heraus, dazu Herr Boehme der nicht selbst Auctor der Uebersetzung ist, eine Vorrede und Dedication gemacht. Das 2. Volumen kam 1714 zum Vorschein. Bey der Uebersetzung des ersten Vol. hatte sich der Auctor zu viel Freyheit gebraucht, und mehr eine paraphrasin, als Version, gegeben. Daher Herr Boehme nachgehends bey der andern Auflage 1720 die Version nach dem Original revidirte." *Erbauliche Schriften*, I, 48.]

Leibniz, Gottfried Wilhelm. A Letter . . . to the author of the Reflections on the origin of Mahometanism. [In Reeland, Adrian, *Of the Mahometan Religion*, Pt. 3.]

1714

Arndt, Johann. Of True Christianity. London. [See note to 1712 edition]

Cramer, Joannes Fridericus. The Funeral Elogy and character of . . . the late Princess Sophia. Translated [from the Latin] into English . . . by Mr. Toland. London.

1715

King, John. A royal compleat Grammar, English and High German. Das ist: eine königliche volkommene Grammatica. London. B. Barker & C. King.

1716

Arndt, Johann. The Garden of Paradise: or, Holy prayers and exercises. Pursuing the design of the famous treatise of True Christianity. Now done into English. [Translation revised and corrected by Anton Wilhelm Boehm]. J. Downing. London.

Francke, August Hermann. Three practical discourses: I. Of the love of God. II. Of charity to the poor. III. Of the differing degrees of glory. By August. Herman. Franck. Done into English from the High-Dutch. London. Printed and sold by J. Downing.

Francke, August Hermann. Pietas Hallensis; or an abstract of the marvellous foot-steps of divine providence. Part 3. To which is prefix'd a Letter of the author to a Reverend Divine in New-England. [Cotton Mather]. London. [According to LC, Part 2 was also printed in 1716.]

King, John. A compleat English guide for High Germans. 2nd ed. London.

Pufendorf, Samuel. Of the law of nature and of nations. Translated by J. Spavan. 2 Vol. Printed for T. Varnan. London.

Pufendorf, Samuel. The Whole duty of Man according to the Law of Nature. 4th ed. with the notes of Mr. Barbeyrac, and many other additions and amendments. By A. Tooke. London.

1717

Agricola, Georg Andreas. The Artificial Gardener; being a discovery of a new invention for the sudden growth of all sorts of trees and plants. Translated from the High-Dutch . . . by a Fellow of the Royal Society. E. Curll. London.

Culmann, Leonhard. Sentences for children, English and Latin. For the first entrers into Latin. Translated by Charles Hoole. Printed in London by Stationers.

Leibniz, Gottfried Wilhelm. A Collection of Papers, which passed between the late learned Mr. Leibnitz, and Dr. Clarke, in the years 1715 and 1716 relating to the Principles of Natural Philosophy and Religion. With an appendix. To which are added, Letters to Dr. Clarke concerning liberty and necessity; from a gentleman of the University of Cambridge [i.e. John Bulkeley]: with the Doctor's answers to them. Also, remarks upon a book, entituled, A Philosophical Enquiry concerning Human Liberty [by Anthony Collins]. By Samuel Clarke. 2 pt. James Knapton. London.

1719
Pufendorf, Samuel. An introduction to the history of the principal states of Europe. 8th ed. London.
Pufendorf, Samuel. Of the relation between Church and State. London.

1720
Arndt, Johann. Of true Christianity. Now revised. The second edition. 2 Volumes. Booth & Co. London. [Volume 1 only is of the 2nd edition. Volume 2 is a duplicate of the corresponding volume of the 1714 edition. See note 1712 edition.]
The German Rogue: or the life and merry adventures, cheats, stratagems and contrivances of Tiel Eulenspiegle. Made English from the High-Dutch. London.
Jacobi, Johann Christian. A collection of divine hymns, translated from the High Dutch. Together with their proper tunes and thorough bass. London.

1721
Agricola, Georg Andreas. A Philosophical Treatise of Husbandry and Gardening. Translated from the High-Dutch [by H. G.]. Revised by R. Bradley. P. Vaillant, W. Mears, and F. Clay. London.

1722
Jacobi, Johann Christian. Psalmodia Germanica; or, a specimen of Divine Hymns. Translated from the High Dutch. Together with their proper tunes and thorough bass. J. Young. London.

1723
Lange, Lorenz. Laurence Lange's Journey from Petersbourg to Peking. In *The Present state of Russia* Vol. 2. London.
The most Pleasing and Delightful History of Reynard the fox. To which is added the History of Cawwood the Rook. 5th ed. T. Norris. London.

1725
Jacobi, Johann Christian. Psalmodia Germanica. Part 2. London.
A view of London and Westminster: or, the town spy. London. [See Morgan SA-564-1].

1726
Muralt, Beat Ludwig von. Letters describing the character and customs of the English and French Nations. With a curious essay on travelling. And a criticism [Eng. and Fr.] on Boileau's Description of Paris. The second edition. To which are now added, Critical Remarks on the whole work by gentlemen of the English and French nations. Translated from the French. 2 pt. T. Edlin. London.

1727
Comenius, Johann Amos. Sensualium pictus, or a picture and nomenclature of all the chief things that are in the world . . . written by the author in Latin and High Dutch and translated into English by Charles Hoole. London.
Francke, August Hermann. Pietas Hallensis; or, a publick demonstration of the footsteps of a divine being yet in the world: in an historical narration of the Orphan House. Edinburgh.
The Surprising Life and Death of Doctor J. Faustus. To which is now added, the Necromancer; or, Harlequin, Doctor Faustus. Likewise, The whole Life of Fryar Bacon. Truly translated from the original copies. Printed and sold by the Booksellers. London.

1728
Culmann, Leonhard. Sentences for children, English and Latin. Translated by Charles Hoole. Printed in London by Stationers.

1729

Pufendorf, Samuel. Of the law of nature and of nations. Fourth edition . . . corrected. To which is now prefixed, Mr. Barbeyrac's Prefatory Discourse. Done into English by Mr. Carew. London.

1730

Behrens, Georg Henning. The natural history of Hartz-Forest, in His Majesty King George's German dominions. [Translated by J. Andree.] T. Osborne. London.

Boehme, Jacob. The Four Complexions: or, a Treatise of consolatory instruction. [Translated by John Sparrow. The preface is reprinted from that prefixed to C. Hotham's translation, 1654.] J. Scott. London. [date?]

Divine Hymns of love and praise . . . printed in Philadelphia by Benjamin Franklin. [Commissioned by the Monastery of Ephrata].

1731

Beiler, Benedictus. A New German Grammar . . . to which are added several useful and familiar dialogues. The Author. London.

Francke, August Hermann. Nicodemus: or a treatise against the fear of man. Done into English [by Anton Wilhelm Boehm] 2nd ed. Edinburgh.

Kolb, Peter. The present State of the Cape of Good Hope, or a particular account of the several nations of the Hottentots . . . with a short account of the Dutch settlement at the Cape. Written originally in High German. Done into English . . . by Mr. [Guido] Medley: Illustrated with copper plates. W. Innys. London. 2 Vols.

1732

Baumgarten, zu Breitenbach, Martin von. The travels of Martin Baumgarten . . . through Egypt, Arabia, Palestine and Syria, with the author's life done out of Latin [by C. Donauer]. In Churchill, A. & J., *Collections of Voyages and Travels*, I. London.

Eisenmenger, Johann Andreas. The traditions of the Jews: with the expositions and doctrines of the Rabbins. Translated [by Rev. John Peter Stehelin] from the High Dutch. 2 Vols. London. Printed for G. Smith . . . and sold by J. Brotherton . . . and Stephen Austen. [A serial publication. See Wiles, R.M., p. 283].

Francke, August Hermann. Christus Sacrae Scripturae Nucleus: or Christ the sum and substance of the Holy Scriptures in the Old and New Testament. Written in German . . . now rendered into English, by an antient Doctor of Physick. London.

Jacobi, Johann Christian. Psalmodia Germanica: or, the German psalmody. Translated from the High Dutch. Together with their proper tunes and thorough bass. 2nd ed. Corrected and enlarged. London. Printed by G. Smith.

Wagener, Zacharias. A short account of the Voyages of Z. Wagener perform'd in thirty-five years. Translated from the High Dutch. In Churchill's *Collection of Voyages and Travels*, Vol. 2. London.

1733

History of Dr. John Faustus, from his birth to his death. With the history of Friar Bacon, magician of England, and the lives of conjurers Bungey and Vandermast. Truly translated from the original. With cuts. Boston. Printed by T. Fleet.

1734

Eisenmenger, Johann Andreas. The traditions of the Jews. Vol. 2. London.

Pöllnitz, Karl Ludwig. Memoirs. Translated [from the French] by S. Whatley. London.

Reck, Philip Georg von. An Extract of the Journals of Mr. Commissary v. Reck, who conducted the first transport of Saltzburgers to Georgia; and of the Reverend Mr. Boltzius, one of their ministers. Giving an account of their voyage to, and happy settlement in that province. Christian Knowledge Society. London.

1735

Francke, August Hermann. The whole duty of man according to the Law of Nature. 5th ed. R. Gosling. London.

The most pleasing and delightful history of Reynard the fox. 6th ed. London.

Rambach, Johann Jacob. Memoirs of the life and death of the late Reverend Mr. Anthony William Boehm. Made English by John Christian Jacobi. London.

1736

Strahlenberg, Philip Johan. An histori-geographical description of the north and eastern parts of Europe and Asia; but more particularly of Russia, Siberia, and Great Tartary both in their ancient and modern state: together with an entire new polyglot table of the dialects of 32 Tartarian nations. Faithfully translated into English. London.

1737

Mascov, Johann Jakob. The history of the ancient Germans and other ancient northern nations, who overthrew the Roman Empire, and established that of the Germans, and most of the Kingdoms of Europe. Translated into English by Thomas Lediard. 2 Vols. London.

Pöllnitz, Karl Ludwig von. Les Amusements des Spa: or the Gallantries of the Spaw in Germany. London.

Pöllnitz, Karl Ludwig von. The Memoirs of Charles-Lewis, Baron de Pöllnitz, being observations he made in his late travels from Prussia thro' Germany, Italy, France, Flanders, Holland, England . . . in letters to his friend. Discovering not only the present state of the chief cities and towns; but the characters of the principal persons at the several courts. London. [1737-38]

Wesley, John. Collection of Psalms and Hymns. Charles-Town. Printed by Lewis Timothy.

Wohlfahrt, Michael. The wisdom of God crying and calling to the sons and daughters of men for repentance. Being the testimony deliver'd to the people in Philadelphia Market, Sept., 1734, by Michael Wellfare; together with some additional remarks on the present state of Christianity in Pennsylvania. Philadelphia. Printed and sold by Benjamin Franklin.

1738

Pöllnitz, Karl Ludwig von. The memoirs of Charles Lewis, Baron de Pöllnitz. Translated by Stephen Whatley. 5 Vols. Dublin.

Rauwolff, Leonhardt. Travels through the Low Countries. Dr. L. Rauwolff's journey into the Eastern countries. Translated from the original High-Dutch by N. Staphorst. 2. Vols. London.

Strahlenberg, Philip Johann. An histori-geographical description of the north and eastern parts of Europe and Asia; but more particularly of Russia, Siberia, and Great Tartary both in their ancient and modern state: together with an entire new polyglot table of the dialects of 32 Tartarian nations. Faithfully translated into English. London.

Wesley, John. A collection of psalms and hymns. London.

1739

Dedekind, Friedrich. Grobianus; or, the Compleat Booby. An ironical poem. In three books. Done into English from the original Latin of Friderich Dedekindus, by Roger Bull. T. Cooper. London. [also 2nd ed. in 1739]

Pöllnitz, Karl Ludwig von. The memoirs of Charles-Lewis Baron de Pöllnitz. [Translated by Stephen Whatley] 2nd ed. with additions. 2 Vols. D. Browne. London.

Wesley, John and Charles. Hymns and sacred poems. Printed by William Strahan; sold by James Hutton and at Mr. Bray's. London. [three eds. in 1739]

1740

Francke, August Hermann. A letter concerning the most useful Way of Preaching. Written in German . . . translated into Latin . . . and out of the Latin into English by David Jennings. [See Evans, 4534]

Pöllnitz, Karl Ludwig von. Les Amusements de Spa: or, The Gallantries of the Spaw in Germany. Containing the virtues of every spring; their nature and several uses. The reasons why frequented by persons of the first distinctions; besides drinking the waters. The various diversions and amusements of the place. Many entertaining histories of the principal persons resorting to the Spaw. Translated into English from the French original. 2nd ed. Dublin. Printed for J. Kelburn.

The right pleasant and diverting history of Fortunatus, and his two Sons. 11th ed. Now published in English, by T. [Churchyard]. London.

The surprising life . . . of Doctor J. Faustus. London. (See 1727 ed. Date?]

Wesley, John and Charles. Hymns and sacred poems. Published by John Wesley, M. A. Fellow of Lincoln College, Oxford, and Charles Wesley, M. A. Student of Christ-Church, Oxford. Philadelphia: Printed by Andrew and William Bradford, and sold for the benefit of the poor in Georgia. [also printed in London]

Zinzendorf, Ludwig. Sixteen discourses on the redemption of man by the death of Christ, preached at Berlin by the Right Reverend and Most Illustrious Count Zinzendorf, Bishop of the Ancient Moravian Church. Translated from the High Dutch. With a dedication to the Archbishops, Bishops, and Clergy, giving some account of the Moravian Brethren. London.

1741

Acta Germanica; or, the Literary memoirs of Germany. Done from the Latin and High-Dutch, by a Society of Gentlemen. London. [serial ed. See Wiles, 326].

A collection of hymns for the Moravian Brethren. London. ["Until this date (1742) two English Moravian hymn-books had been published. The first was put to press Oct. 24, 1741, and was ready for use Nov. 24. It consisted almost exclusively of translations from the German. The second left the press Aug. 4, 1742. This had some English hymns in addition to the contents of the first edition." Julian, 767]

Gerhard, Johann. Free grace in truth. The XXIVth meditation of Dr. John Gerhard: translated from Latin into English. With notes for the better understanding the author's meaning. Philadelphia. Printed and sold by Benjamin Franklin.

The Groans of Germany; or, the enquiry of a Protestant German into the original cause of the present distractions of the Empire. Translated from the original lately published at the Hague. London. [At least six editions in 1741]

Luther, Martin. A commentary on St. Paul's epistle to the Galatians. London. [See Wiles, 329. This was No. 1 of a serial publication in *Scots Magazine*.]

Wesley, John and Charles. A collection of psalms and hymns. [See Julian, 1259]

1742

A collection of hymns with several translations from the hymn-book of the Moravian Brethren. London.

Francke, August Hermann. A continuation of the Account of the Orphan House in Georgia [by George Whitefield] to which are also subjoined some extracts from an account of a work of a like nature carried on by the late Professor Franck. Edinburgh.

Hübner, Johann. The historical companion: being a new introduction to the political history of all nations . . . from the earliest ages to the present time. Written originally in High-Dutch. By Mr. John Hubner for the use of schools. And now faithfully translated into English. London. Printed for G. Smith.

A Manual of Doctrine; or, a second essay to bring into the form of question and answer as well the fundamental doctrines, as the other scripture-knowledge, of the Protestant Congregations . . . call'd. The Brethren. Written in High-Dutch, by the author of the first Essay. And now translated into English, with an introduction. J. Hutton. London.

A Short Catechism for some Congregations of Jesus of the Reformed Religion in Pennsylvania who keep to the ancient synod of Bern; agreeable to the doctrine of the Moravian Church. First published in German. Philadelphia. Printed by Isaiah Warner, almost opposite to Charles Brockden's in Chestnut-street.

Wesley, John and Charles. Hymns and sacred poems. [the third collection] Felix Farley. Bristol.

Wesley, John. A collection of German hymns. London. [See Julian, 1259]

Wesley, John. A collection of thirty-six tunes, set to music, as they are sung at the Foundry. London.

Zinzendorf, Ludwig. A compendious extract containing the chiefest articles of doctrine and most remarkable transactions of Count Lewis of Zinzendorff and the Moravians. Collected from the German. Philadelphia.

Zinzendorf, Ludwig. The remarks, which the author of the Compendious Extract etc., in the preface to his book, has friendly desired of the Rev. of Thurenstein, for the time Pastor of the Lutheran Congregation of J.C. in Philadelphia. Philadelphia. Printed and sold by Benjamin Franklin.

Zinzendorf, Ludwig. Seven Sermons on the Godhead of the Lamb; or the divinity of Jesus Christ, by the Right Reverend and most illustrious Count Zinzendorf, Bishop of the Moravian Church. Preached in 1741 just before his second voyage to the West Indies: and translated from the German manuscript. London.

1743

Acta Germanica; or, the literary memoirs of Germany. Done from the Latin and High Dutch by a Society of Gentlemen. Volume I. London.

Cennick, John. Sacred Hymns for the Use of Religious Societies. 3 pt. Felix Farley, Bristol. M. Lewis, London. [1743-64. Pt. 3 printed in London only]

Hutton, James. A Collection of Hyms with several translations from the hymn-book of the Moravian Brethren. 2nd ed. London.

Königsmarck, Marie Aurora Gräfin von. Memoirs of the Love and State-Intrigues of the Court of H[anover] from the Marriage of the Princess of Z[ell], to the death of Count K[önigsmarck]. Written originally in High German by the celebrated Countess of K[önigsmarck]. London.

Popular prejudices concerning partiality to the interests of Hanover, to the subjects of that Electorate, and particularly to the Hanoverian Troops in British pay, freely examined and discussed; in which the conduct of that corps, at Dettingen ... and during the whole late campaign is ... vindicated. In a letter from an officer at Hanover to a Hanoverian nobleman at the Hague. London.

United Brethren or Unitas Fratrum, commonly called Moravians. A choice collection of hymns; with several new translations from the hymn-book of the Moravian Brethren. Philadelphia. Printed by Isaiah Warner and Cornelia Bradford.

Zinzendorf, Ludwig. Every man's right to live. A sermon on Ezek. XXXIII.2. Why will ye die? Preached at Philadelphia, by the Rev. Lewis of Thurenstein, Deacon of the Ancient Moravian Church. Translated from German into English. Philadelphia. Benjamin Franklin.

1744

Arndt, Johann. Of True Christianity. London. [Listed in *A Catalogue of the Library at King's Cliffe*.]

Baumgarten, zu Breitenbach, Martin von. Travels ... through Egypt, Arabia, Palestine, and Syria. [See 1732 ed.]

Francke, August Hermann. Nicodemus; or a treatise on the fear of Man. Abridged by J. Wesley. The third ed. Newcastle upon Tyre.

Francke, August Hermann. Nicodemus; or, a treatise against the fear of man. Translated from the High Dutch. 3rd ed. Boston.

Friedrich II. A view of the motives which have obliged the King ... to grant auxiliary unto his imperial majesty. London.

Königsmarck, Marie Aurora Gräfin von. A Home Truth; being memoirs of the love and state-intrigues of the court of H[anover]; from the marriage of the Princess of Z[ell], to the . . . death of Count K[önigsmark]. Written originally in High-German by . . . Countess of K[önigsmark]. 2nd ed. London. [date?]

Leibniz, Gottfried Wilhelm. A Letter from Mr. Leibnitz to Mr. Burnet of Kemney. [24 Aug. 1697] French and English. In L. P. Thueming *A Defence of the late Dr. S. Clarke*, London.

A Letter from Hanover, shewing the true cause of the present broils of Germany and confustions of Europe, and particularly, the probable motives and consequences of the King of Prussia's second invasion of the Austrian territories; with observations on his Prussian Majesty's late manifesto, and the disinclination of the Dutch to declare against France. Done into English from the original High Dutch. London.

Mandelslo, Johann Albrecht von. The Remarks and Observations made by J. A. de Mandelslo in his passage from the kingdom of Persia through several countries of the Indies. Translated from the original. In J. Harris *Navigantium*, Vol. 1. London.

The queen of Hungary's manifesto. Vienna. [See Morgan SA 432-1]

Wagener, Zacharias. A short account of the voyages of Zacharias Wagener. Taken out of his own journal. 3rd ed. London.

The word for the disciples of the God with us for the year 1744. Translated from the German. London. [James Hutton, anon. periodical]

1745

Acta Germanica; or the literary memoirs of Germany. London. [Probably the Volume II of the 1741 serial publication. Number 6 of Volume II is listed in *Gentlemen's Magazine* April 1745 as published (or sold) by Robinson. See Wiles, 344]

Pöllnitz, Karl Ludwig von. The memoirs of Charles-Lewis, Baron de Pöllnitz. [translated by Stephen Whatley from the French] 3rd ed. with additions. 5 Vols. Daniel Browne. London.

The visible pursuit of a foreign interest. London. [See Morgan SA 566-1]

Lange, Lorenz. The travels of L. L. in China, in 1717. Translated from the High Dutch. In *A New General Collection of Voyages and Travels*, Vol. 3.

1746

Beiler, Benedictus. A new German grammar, to which are added some useful and familiar dialogues. Philadelphia, Benjamin Franklin. [First appeared in London in 1731]

Hutton, James. A collection of hymns with several translations from the hymn-book of the Moravian Brethren. 3rd ed. London.

Hutton, James. A collection of hymns consisting chiefly of translations from the German. Part II. London. [These two volumes contain 403 hymns plus a collection of un-numbered hymns and single verses. See Julian, 768]

Ludwig, Christian. Dictionary of High Dutch and English. Philadelphia, Benjamin Franklin. [This is a translation of the *Teutsch-Englisches Lexicon*, Leipzig, 1716. Ludwig also published in 1706 *A Dictionary English, German and French* with later editions in 1736, 1763, and 1791. See Harold Jantz, "Christian Lodowick of Newport and Leipzig," *Rhode Island History*, Oct. 1944 and Jan. 1945.]

Wesley, Charles. Hymns on the great festivals and other occasions. London. [This is the hymn collection for which Johann Friedrich Lampe wrote the music.]

Luther, Martin. Thirty-Four Sermons. S. Powell. Dublin.

Sigfrid, Isaac, and Wyttenbach, Daniel. Theological theses, containing the chief heads of the Christian doctrine reduced from axioms; composed and publickly defended in the presence and under the direction of the very reverend and most judicious John Henry Ringier, V. D. M. and professor of controversial divinity in the Academy at Bern. By Isaac Sigfrid, of Zoffingen in Bern, and Daniel Wyttenbach, of Bern, in order to obtain the honour of the D. Ministry. [Translated from the Latin] Printed and sold by Samuel Brown at the foot of Pot-Baker's Hill, between the New-Dutch Church and Fly-Market, and by Elizabeth Lydekker, in Lary's-Street.

Trenck, Frieherr von. Memoirs of the life of the illustrious Francis Baron Trenck. Written by himself and done from the original German into English. W. Owen. London.

1748

Eisenmenger, Johann Andreas. Rabbinical Literature: or, the Traditions of the Jews, contained in the Talmud and other mystical writings. Likewise the opinions of that people concerning Messiah. With an appendix, comprizing Buxtorf's account of the religious customs and ceremonies of that nation; also a preliminary enquiry into the origin, progress, authority, and usefulness of these traditions. By the Rev'd Mr. J. P. Stehelin. [i.e. a translation of *Entdecktes Judenthum* by Eisenmenger, with a preface by Stehelin] 2 Vols. J. Robinson. London.

Friedrich II. Memoirs of the House of Brandenburg. Translated from the original. London.

"Huffumbourghausen, Baron." The Congress of the Beasts . . . for negotiating a peace between . . . the quadrupedes at war. A farce of two acts. Written originally in High Dutch. Translated by J.J. Heidegger. To which is prefixt a curious print of the last scene . . . by an eminent hand. London. [A satire on the congress at Aix-la-Chapelle. At least 7 editions in London in 1748 plus at least 2 in America. The 7th edition London, said to be "inrich'd with critical and explanatory matter, by the author." Morgan, S 4629-1.] [actually a translation?]

Hutton, James. A collection of hymns with several translations from the hymn-book of the Moravian Brethren. Part III. London.

Pöllnitz, Ludwig von. The amusements of Aix-la-Chapelle. [Possibly related to Amussements des eaux d' Aix-la-Chapelle, 3 Vols. (Amsterdam, 1736). See Wiles, 354]

Pufendorf, Samuel. An introduction to the history of the principal states of Europe. Begun by Baron Pufendorf and continued down to . . . 1743, by M. Martinière. Improved from the French by James Sayer. 2 Vols. London.

1749

Arndt, Johann. Of true Christianity. Published in *A Christian Library*, 50 Volumes edited by John Wesley, Bristol, 1749-55.

Augsburg Confession. [Published by the Moravians. See 1755 edition, and Evans, 7262] London.

Francke, August Hermann. Nicodemus; or a treatise on the fear of man. Written in German by A. H. Franck. Abridged by John Wesley. 4th ed. Dublin.

Francke, August Hermann. Nicodemus. [also published by John Wesley in *A Christian Library*]

Hutton, James. A collection of hymns with several translations from the hymn-book of the Moravian Brethren. Part III, 2nd ed. London.

Pufendorf, Samuel. Of the law of nature and of nations. 5th ed. Carefully corrected. To which is prefix'd M. Barbeyrac's prefatory Discourse done into English by Mr. Carew. London.

Wesley, John. Hymns extracted from the Brethren's book. London.

Zinzendorf, Ludwig. An account of the doctrine, manners, liturgy, and idiom of the Unitas Fratrum. Taken from the Acta Fratrum Unitatis in Anglia. With a translation of the Enchiridion Theologiae Patristicae by Bishop Gambold. London.

Zinzendorf, Ludwig. Hymns composed for the use of the Brethren. By the right reverend and most illustrious C. Z. Published for the benefit of all mankind in the year 1749.

1750

The history of Doctor J. Faustus. Shewing, how he sold himself to the devil . . . for 24 years . . . how the devil came for him, and tore him to pieces. London.

The history of Fortunatus, containing various surprising adventures . . . a purse that could not be emptied. London. [date?]

The History of Reynard the fox. Printed and sold in Aldermary Church Yard, Bow Lane. London.

Pöllnitz, Karl Ludwig von. La Saxe galante; or, the amorous adventures of Frederick Augustus II. Translated from the French by a gentleman of Oxford. London. [date?]

Wolff, Christian Freiherr von. The real happiness of a People under a philosophical king demonstrated; not only from the nature of things, but from the undoubted experience of the Chinese under . . . Fohi. London.

1751

Friedrich II. Memoirs of the house of Brandenburg. London.

Zinzendorf, Ludwig. Maxims, theological ideas and sentences, out of the present Ordinary of the Brethren's Churches, his dissertations and discources from the year 1738 till 1747. Extracted by J. Gambold, M. A. with a Letter from the author annex'd. London.

Zinzendorf, Ludwig. Sixteen discourses on Jesus Christ our Lord. Being an exposition of the second part of the Creed. Preached at Berlin by the Right Reverend Lewis, Bishop of the Brethren's Church. 2nd ed. London.

1752

Bachmair, John James. A Complete German Grammar. In two parts. 2nd ed. Linde. London.

Baumgarten, zu Breitenbach, Martin von. Travels . . . through Egypt, Arabia, Palestine, and Syria. London.

Boehme, Jacob. The Way to Christ discovered. Joseph Harrop. Manchester. [The translations are generally those published in 1648. The epistle of 20 April, 1624, is translated by Ellistone. BM]

Gellert, Christian Fürchtegott. History of the Swedish countess of Guildenstern. Dodsley. London.

Hutton, James. Some other hymns and poems, consisting chiefiy of translations from the German. London.

Wagener, Zacharias. A short account of the voyages of Zacharias Wagener. [same as 1744 ed. See Morgan 9617.]

1753

Bucer, Martin. The judgement of Martin Bucer concerning divorce. Translated by John Milton. [published in *Works*, I. See Morgan 815.]

Frey, Andrew. A true and authentic account of Andrew Frey; containing the occasion of his coming among the Herrnhuters or Moravians, his observations on their conferences . . . and the reasons for which he left them, and his motives for publishing this account. Translated from the German. London.

Friedrich II. Sylla, a dramatic entertainment presented . . . 27th March, 1753. Translated from the French by Mr. Derrick. London.

Friedrich II. Letters to the Public by His Majesty the King of Prussia. Translated from the original edition. W. Owen. London.

K., M. The Fatal consequences of the unscriptural doctrine of predestination and reprobation; with a caution against it. Written in High-Dutch by M. K. and translated an [sic] desire. Germantown. Christopher Sowr.

Klein-Nicolai, Georg. The everlasting Gospel commanded to be preached by Jesus Christ, Judge of the living and dead, unto all creatures, Mark xvi. 15. Concerning the eternal redemption found out by him, whereby devil, sin, hell, and death shall at last be abolished, and the whole creation restored to its primative purity; being a testimony against the present anti-christian world. Written in German by Paul Siegvolck, and translated into English by John S[echla]. Christopher Sower.

126

Rimius, Heinrich. A Candid Narrative of the rise and progress of the Herrnhuters, commonly call'd Moravians or Unitas Fratrum; with a short account of their doctrines, observations on their politics in general and particularly on their conduct in the County of Büdingen in Germany. London.

Zinzendorf, Ludwig. Twenty-one Discourses or dissertations upon the Augsburg-Confession, which is also the Brethren's confession of faith. To which is prefixed a Synodal writing on the same subject. Translated by F. Okeley. London.

1754

Baumgarten, Sigmund Jakob. A supplement to the English Universal History, from the German. Lynde. London.

Bogatzky, Karl Heinrich. A Golden Treasury for the Children of God, whose treasure is in heaven; consisting of select texts of the Bible, with ... observations ... for every day in the year. Translated from the 19th edition of the German. A. Linde. London. [77 editions of this translation were published before 1925. Morgan 614]

Francke, August Hermann. A letter concerning the most useful way of Preaching. Written in the German language ... Translated into Latin ... and out of the Latin into English by David Jennings. London.

Gambold, John. A collection of Hymns for the Children of God in all ages, from the beginning till now. In two parts. Designed chiefly for the use of the congregations in union with the Brethren's church. At the Brethren's Chapel. London.

The History of the Moravians from their first Settlement at Herrnhaag in the County of Büdingen down to the present Time; with a view chiefly to their political intrigues. Collected from the public acts of Büdingen and other authentic vouchers. Translated from the German. London.

Loën, Johann. [Lowhen]. The Analysis of Nobility, in its Origin; Translated from the ... German ... with notes. J. Robinson. London.

Select hymns from German psalmody. Tranquebar.

1755

Augsburg Confession. The Whole System of the xxviii Articles of the Evangelical unvaried Confession. Presented at Ausbourgh to the Emperor Charles V. by the Protestant Princes and States. To be compared with the translations of the Moravians, printed at London in the year 1749. [translated by John A. Waygand] J. Parker & W. Weyman. New York.

Engel, Friedirch. A new Theory of Human Nature, with a correspondent system of Education. London.

A letter from a minister of the Moravian branch of the Unitas Fratrum, together with some ... notes by the English editor, to the author of the Moravians compared and detected. London.

Rimius, Heinrich. A Supplement to the Candid Narrative of the rise and progress of the Herrnhuters, commonly called Moravians, or Unitas Fratrum, in which ... the political scheme and artful proceedings of their Patriarch are disclosed. With animadversions on sundry flagrant untruths advanced by Mr. Zinzendorf. London.

Zinzendorf, Ludwig. An exposition, of true state, of the matters objected in England to the people known by the name of Unitas Fratrum. By the Ordinary of the Brethren. With notes and additions by the editor. [James Hutton]. In two parts. London.

1756

Friedrich II. Motives which have obliged His Majesty ... to prevent the designs of the court of Vienna. [French and English] Berlin and London.

The History of Reynard the Fox, Bruin the Bear. London.

Huebner, Johann. Easy introduction to the study of the holy scriptures. Translated by D. Bellamy. London.

Keyssler, Johann Georg. Travels through Germany, Bohemia, Hungary, Switzerland, Italy, and Lorrain. Containing an accurate description of the present state and curiosities of those countries. Translated from the 2nd German edition. 4 Vols. London.

1757
Friedrich II. Memoirs of the House of Brandenburg from the earliest accounts to the death of Frederic I. King of Prussia. To which are added four dissertations . . . and a preliminary discourse. 2 pt. J. Nourse. London.

Gellert, Christian Fürchtegott. History of the Swedish countess of Guildenstern. 2 parts. J. Scott. London.

Hentzner, Paul. A journey into England in the year 1598. [being a part of the ininerary of P. H. translated by R. Bentley. Edited by Horace Walpole, Earl of Oxford] Latin and English. Strawberry Hill.

Rabener, Gottlieb Wilhelm. Satirical Letters. Translated from the German of G. W. Rabener. 2 Vols. A. Linde. London.

Weiser, Conrad. Translation of a German letter, wrote [1746] by Conrad Weiser, Esq., interpreter, on Indian affairs, for the Province of Pennsylvania. Benjamin Franklin and D. Hall. Philadelphia.

1758
Fraenckel, David Ben Naphtali Hirsch. A Thanksgiving sermon, for the important and astonishing victory obtain'd on the fifth of December, 1757. By the glorious King of Prussia, over the united, and far superior forces of the Austrians in Silesia. Preach'd on the Sabbath of the tenth of said month at the Synagogue of the Jews, in Berlin. Translated from the German original, printed at Berlin. The ninth edition. London and Boston. Reprinted and sold by Green and Russell at their Printing Office in Queen-Street. [a 10th ed. also in 1758]

Friedrich II. An epistle . . . to M. Voltaire. [translated from French] London. [a 2nd edition also in 1758]

Friedrich II. The king of Prussia's criticism on the Henriad of Monsieur de Voltaire, translated from the original. With a preface, containing a short account of the disgrace & retreat of that favorite. J. Rivington. London.

Friedrich II. The life and actions of Frederic the victorious king of Prussia. Compiled from original memoirs and documents. London.

Friedrich II. Memoirs of the House of Brandenburg. To which are added four dissertations. London.

Friedrich II. Memoirs of the House of Brandenburg. 3rd ed. Dublin.

Friedrich II. An ode . . . after the victory at Rosbach. Translated . . . with the original French on the opposite pages. London.

Friedrich II. The relaxation of war. A poem . . . written by his Majesty. [French and English] London.

Friedrich II. The relaxation of war, or, the hero's philosophy. A poem. [French and English] Philadelphia and New York.

Keyssler, Johann Georg. Travels through Germany, Hungary, Bohemia, Switzerland, Italy, and Lorrain. To which is prefixed the life of the author by . . . G. Schutze. Translated from . . . the German. 4 Vols. London. [Vol. 4 contains a MS Index]

Winkler, Johann Heinrich. Elements of natural philosophy. London.

1759
Bogatzky, Karl. Edifying Thoughts on God's Paternal Heart, and the Lord's Prayer. Translated from the German. A. Linde. London.

Friedrich II. An authentic account of the barbarity of the Russians before and after the King of Prussia's victory over them, near Zaindorff. Extracted from two letters wrote originally in German by him, Oct. 1758. Recommended by the Rev. Mr. Whitefield. From the Edinburgh third edition. Boston, N. E. Reprinted by S. Kneeland.

The litany-book, according to the manner of singing at present mostly in use among the

Brethren, again revised and in this convenient form set forth by the Brethren's chantor. From the 4th German edition. London.

Rambach, Johann Jacob. Considerations on the sufferings of Christ. London.

1760

Baumgarten, Sigmund Jakob. A Supplement to the English Universal History. From the German. Lynde. London.

Keyssler, Johann Georg. Travels through Germany giving a true and just description of the present state of those countries. Illustrated with copper plates, engraved from drawings taken on the spot. Carefully translated from the second edition of the German. The third edition. 4 Vols. For G. Keith. London.

Luther, Martin. A Commentary on St. Paul's Epistle to the Galatians. Written by the Famous Champion of the Faith of Christ, Dr. Martin Luther. [With the text] M. Lewis. London.

Madan, Martin. A Collection of Psalms and Hymns, extracted from various authors, and published by the Reverend Mr. Madan. London. [For a history of this collection see Julian, 710.]

Rambach, Johann Jacob. Pious Aspirations for the use of devout communicants . . . founded on the history of the Sufferings of Christ, as related by the four Evangelists. Extracted from . . . J. Rambach . . . by George Whitefield. London.

1761

Bogatzky, Karl. Edifying thoughts on God's paternal heart. J. Richardson and T. Field. London.

Friedrich II. The 7th epistle attempted in English from the King of Prussia's Oeuvres du Philosophe de Sans Souci, to Maupertuis. London.

Gessner, Salomon. The Death of Abel, in five books, attempted from the German of Mr. Gessner [by Mrs. Mary Collyer]. London.

Gessner, Salomon. The Death of Abel. [Review with lengthy excerpts in *Annual Register*, 4 (1761). See Morgan 2259]

Kelpius, Johannes. A short, easy, and comprehensive method of prayer. Translated from the German [by C. Witt]. And published for a father [sic] promotion, knowledge and benefit of inward prayer. By a Lover of Internal
Devotion. Philiadelphia. Printed by Henry Miller, in Second-street, next to the corner of Race-street.

Luther, Martin. The small catechism of Dr. Martin Luther, translated into English by Rev. C. M. Wrangel. Philadelphia. Printed by Henry Miller.

Mueller, Gerhard Friedrich. Voyages from Asia to America for completing the Discoveries of the North-West coast of America. To which is prefixed, a summary of the Voyages made by the Russians on the Frozen Sea, in search of a North-East Passage. Translated from the High Dutch of S. [or rather G. F.] Müller. With the addition of three new maps. By T. Jefferys. London.

1762

Bogatzky, Karl. A Golden Treasury for the Children of God, whose treasure is in heaven; consisting of select texts of the Bible, with . . . observations . . . for every day in the year. J. Richardson & T. Field. London.

Büsching, A. F. A New System of Geography: in which is given, a general account of . . . the several kingdoms and states in the known world. Translated [by P. Murdoch] from the last edition of the German original. [a translation of the European portion of the Geography] To the author's discourse are added three essays [by the translator] relative to the subject, illustrated with thirty-six maps. 6 Vols. A Millar. London.

Francke, August Hermann. The holy and sure way of faith of an evangelical Christian. Philadelphia: Printed by H. Miller. [Printed in German and English, in opposite columns.]

Friedrich II. Military Instructions . . . written by the king of Prussia, for the Generals of his Army: Translated by an Officer. London.

Friedrich II. Anti-Machiavel. [In *The Works of N. Machiavel*. Translated by Ellis Farneworth. I, 467-703. London. See Morgan 1987]

Gessner, Salomon. The Death of Abel. 2nd ed. London.

Gessner, Salomon. The Death of Abel. In five books. Philadelphia. Printed by William Bradford.

Gessner, Salomon. The Death of Abel. Boston. Reprinted by Fowle & Draper.

Gessner, Salomon. The Death of Abel. 3rd. ed. R. & J. Dodsley. London.

Gessner, Salomon. Pastorals. London.

Gessner, Salomon. Rural Poems. Translated from the original German, of M. Gessner. Printed for T. Becket, and P. A. De Hondt. London.

Gessner, Salomon. Select Poems from Mr. Gessner's Pastorals. By the Versifier of Anningait and Ajutt [Anne Penny]. London. [a 2nd ed. also in 1762]

Gessner, Salomon. The Thanksgiving Song of Adam, on his recovery from a sickness. Translated by S. Boyce. London.

Rabener, Wilhelm. The employment of souls after separation from the body: a dream. Lownds.

1763

Fraenckel, David Ben Naphaali Hirsch. A thanksgiving sermon. [See 1758 ed.]

Gessner, Salomon. The Death of Abel. 5th ed. London.

Gessner, Salomon. The Death of Abel. Attempted in the style of Milton. By Rev. T. Newcombe. London. [Also printed in Dublin]

Jerusalem, Johann Friedrich Wilhelm. The life of Prince Albert Henry, of Brunswick Luneburg, . . . written originally in German. J. Curtis. London.

Kelpius, Johannes. A short, easy, and comprehensive method of prayer published for a farther promotion, knowledge and benefit of inward prayer. By a Lover of Internal Devotion. The 2nd edition with additions. Germantown. Printed by Christopher Sower. [See 1761 ed.]

Klopstock, Friedrich Gottlieb. The Death of Adam; a tragedy, in three acts. [verse], From the German [by Robert Lloyd]. London.

Klopstock, Friedrich Gottlieb. The Messiah. Attempted from the German of Mr. Klopstock [by Joseph Collyer]. To which is prefix'd his introduction on divine poetry. 2 Vols. London.

Lange, Lorenz. Journal of the residence of Mr. de Lange at the Court of Pekin . . . 1721-1722. [In Bell, J., *Travels*, II, 169-321. See Morgan 5569]

Rambach, Johann Jacob. Meditations and Contemplations on the Sufferings of our Lord and Saviour Jesus Christ. In which the History of the Passion, as given by the four Evangelists, is connected, harmonised, and explained. With suitable prayers and offices of devotion. To which is prefixed a recommendatory preface by P. Fresenius. Translated from the last edition of the German. Illustrated. 2 Vols. London.

United Brethren. A hymn-book for the children belonging to the Brethren's congregations. Taken chiefly out of the German little book. In three books. Philadelphia. Printed [by Henry Miller].

1764

Boehme, Jacob. The works of Jacob Behmen . . . to which is prefixed the life of the author. With figures, illustrating his principles, left by the Reverend William Law. [Edited by G. Ward and T. Langcake. With a portrait. The translations, except in the case of the "Weg zu Christo," where the version from the 1775 edition has been used, are those by J. Sparrow, J. Ellistone and H. Blunden, with the phraseology occasionally slightly altered.] 4 Vols. M. Richardson. London. I 1764, II 1763 [sic], III 1772, IV 1781.

The Heidelbergh catechism or method of instruction, in the Christian religion, as the same is taught in the Reformed Churches and schools of Holland. Translated [from

German] for the use of the Reformed Protestant Dutch Church, of the City of New-York. New York. Printed and sold by John Holt.

Meier, Georg Friedrich. The merry philosopher; or, thoughts on jesting. Containing rules by which a proper judgement of jests may be found, and the criterion for distinguishing true and genuine wit. Together with instuctions for ... those who have a natural turn for pleasantry. Translated into English from the German. 2 Vols. London.

Mueller, Gerhard Friedrich. Voyages from Asia to America. 2nd ed. [See 1761 edition]

Pufendorf, Samuel. An introduction to the history of the principal states of Europe. Continued ... by M. Martiniere. Improved from the French by J. Sayer. 2 Vols. London.

Saalfeld, Adam Friedrich Wilhelm. A Philosophical Discourse on the nature of Dreams. Translated from the German. London.

Schönaich, Christoph Otto. Arminius; or Germania freed. Translated from the 3rd edition of the German original by Baron Cronzeck [or rather, Schönaich]. With an historical and critical preface, by Professor Gottsched. 2 Vols. London.

Wieland, Christoph Martin. The Trial of Abraham. Becket & De Hondt. London.

1765

Bachmair, John James. A complete German Grammar. [Printed in America. See Zeydel, 326]

Beissel, Johann Conrad. A Dissertation on mans fall, translated from the High-German original. Ephrata. Sold at Philadelphia by Messieuis Christoph Marshal and William Dunlap.

Bogatzky, Karl. The important question: What do I lack? London.

Bruehl, Heinrich von. The Life and Character ... of Count Bruhl ... in a series of letters ... carefully translated from the German original [variously ascribed to J. H. G. von Justi and J. C. Adelung]. M. Cooper & C. G. Seyffert. London. [date?]

Gessner, Salomon. The Death of Abel. 7th ed. London.

Gessner, Salomon. The Death of Abel. London, Printed: New-York, Reprinted, by H. Gaine, at the Bible and Crown, in Hanover-Square.

The Heidelberg Catechism, in English. Translated from the German, for the use of the reformed and other schools. Philadelphia. Printed by Anthony Armbruster.

Huebner, Johann. Hubner's Historys of the Bible translated in the English and French tongue. German, English, & French. Hamburg.

Jacobi, Johann Christian. Psalmodia Germanica; or the German Psalmody. Translated from the High German [by J. C. Jacobi]. Together with their proper tunes, and thorough bass. The third edition, corrected and very much enlarged. London and New York. [This edition was prepared by Johann Haberkorn.]

Meier, Georg Friedrich. The merry philosopher; or, thoughts on jesting. [A duplicate of the 1764 ed. with a different title page.] London.

Möser, Justus. Letter to the Rev. Vicar of Savoy. Translated by J.A.F. Warnecke. London.

Winckelmann, Johann Joachim. A description of the famous marble trunk of Hercules, dug up at Rome, commonly called the torso of Belvedere; wroght by Apollonius the son of Nestor, and universally allowed to have been made for a statue of Hercules spinning. Translated from the German of the Abbé Winckelmann by Henry Fusle. London.

Winckelmann, Johann Joachim. Observations on the influence of the different climates upon the polite arts; taken from a history of the fine arts, by the Abbé Winckelmann, librarian at the Vatican, and antiquary to the Pope. London.

Winckelmann, Johann Joachim. Reflections on the Painting and sculpture of the Greeks; with instructions for the connoisseur, and an Essay on Grace in the works of art; translated from the German of the Abbé Winckelmann, librarian of the Vatican ... by Henry Fusseli. London.

1766

Gessner, Salomon. The Death of Abel. 7th ed. New York. Printed by Hugh Gaine.

Klopstock, Friedrich Gottlieb. The Messiah. Attempted from the German of Mr. Klopstock. To which is prefix'd his Introduction on Divine Poetry. The second edition. 2 Vols. London. Printed for J. Dodsley.

Madan, Martin. A Collection of Hymns, for social worship. Extracted from various authors, and published by the Revd. Mr. Madan, and the Revd. Mr. Whitefield. Philadelphia. Printed by W. and T. Bradford.

Möser, Justus. Harlequin; or, a defence of grotesque-comic performances. Translated from the German by J. A. F. Warnecke.

Reimarus, H. S., i.e. Johan Albert Heinrich. Principal truths of natural religion defended and illustrated. Translated by Wynne. London. [See Morgan 7377]

Winckelmann, Johann Joachim. Reflections concerning the imitation of the Grecian artists in painting and sculpture. In a series of letters. Glasgow.

1767

Bodmer, Johann Jacob. Noah; attempted from the German . . . in twelve books. By Joseph Collyer. 2 Vols. J. Collyer. London. [Also printed in Dublin]

Cranz, David. The History of Greenland: containing a description of the country, and its inhabitants; and particularly, a relation of the Mission, carried on for above these thirty years by the Unitas Fratrum, at New Herrnhuth and Lichtenfels, in that Country. Translated from the High-Dutch, and illustrated with maps and other copper-plates. [Edited and in part translated by John Gambold.] 2 Vols. Printed for the Brethren's Society for the Furtherance of the Gospel among the Heathen. London.

Gessner, Salomon. The Death of Abel. A new translation. T. & D. Dodesley. London.

Gessner, Salomon. The Death of Abel. New York. [See Morgan 2269]

The Heidelberg Catechism, or method of instruction in the christian religion as the same is taught in the Reformed Churches and schools of Holland. Translated for the use of the Reformed Protestant Dutch Church, of the city of New-York, examined, compared, and approved by the consistory of the same, and by them recommended for the use of schools and order'd to be printed. The second edition. New York. Printed and sold by John Holt, at the Exchange.

Lessing, Gotthold Ephraim. Laocoön. [See Morgan 5733]

Pfeil, Johann Gottlob. The Memoirs of the Court of P. A Novel, translated by F. W. Streit. 2 Vols.

1768

Bielfeld, Jacob Friedrich. Letters of Baron Bielfeld . . . containing original anecdotes of the Prussian court for the last twenty years. Translated from the German, by Mr. Hooper. 2 Vols. J. Robson; Richardson & Urquhart. London. [See also Morgan S 436-4]

Friedrich II. Elogy on Prince Henry of Prussia. [Translated from the French] London.

Friedrich II. Memoirs of the House of Brandenburg to the death of Frederick William, the present King's father. 2 Vols. J. Nourse. London. [1758-68]

Friedrich II. Royal matins, or, Prussia's public confession, in five mornings. From the French. By a Gentleman of the University of Cambridge. J.Archdeacon. Cambridge.

Gessner, Salomon. The Death of Abel in five books. Attempted from the German of Mr. Gessner. Boston. Printed and sold by Z. Fowle and N. Coverly, in Back-Street. [Dedicated to the Queen and signed Mary Collyer. Not in Evans.]

Gessner, Salomon. Daphnis: a poetical, pastoral novel. Translated . . . by an English Gentleman who resided several years at Hamburgh. To which is prefixed, a prefatory discourse on the origin and use of pastoral poetry. J. Dodsley. London.

Herport, Rev. of Berne. An Essay on truths of importance to the happiness of mankind, wherein the doctrine of oaths . . . is impartially considered. Translated from the German. London.

Mueller, Markus. History of the principal monarchies and states, prior to the Christian era. From the German. Bingley. London. [See Morgan 6525]

Spangenberg, August Gottlieb. A candid declaration of the church of the Unitas Fratrum relative to their labour among the heathen. In the name of the directors of their missions. August Gottlieb Spangenberg. London.

1769

A Collection of Hymns, chiefly extracted from the larger hymn-book of the Brethren's Congregations. London.

Boehme, Jacob. Important Truths relating to spiritual and practical Christianity: selected from several eminent writers. With divers extracts from a treatise, intitled, The Way to Christ, written by Jacob Behmen. Published by a Gentleman retired from business. 4 parts. London.

Klopstock, Friedrich Gottlieb. The Messiah. The fourth edition. 3 Vols. J. Collyer. London.

Michaelis, Johann David. A dissertation on the influence of Opinions on Language, and of Language on Opinions; . . . together with an enquiry into the advantages and practicability of an universal learned language. London.

1770

Bielfeld, Jacob Friedrich. The Elements of Universal Erudition . . . sciences, polite arts, and belles lettres. Translated . . . by W. Hooper. 3 Vols. London.

Bodmer, Johann Jacob. Noah. 2nd ed. 2 Vols. London.

Boehme, Jacob. A Compendious View of the grounds of the Teutonick Philosophy. With considerations by way of enquiry into the . . . writings of J. Behmen. Also several extracts from his writings. Published by a Gentleman retired from Business. 3 parts. Bathurst, Baker. London.

Dell, William. The trial of spirits. As also, Luther's testimony at large upon the whole matter. Hinde. London.

Francke, August Hermann. The holy and sure way of faith of an evangelical Christian. 2nd ed. Philadelphia. Printed and sold by Henry Miller, in Second-Street.

Francke, August Hermann. Nicodemus; or, a treatise against the fear of man. 2nd edition. London.

Friedrich II. Royal mornings. London. [date?]

Gessner, Salomon. The Death of Abel. London Printed; Philadelphia: Re-printed and sold by Joseph Crukshank, and Isaac Collins, in Thirdstreet, opposite the Work-house.

Hirzel, Hans Kaspar. The Rural Socrates, being memoirs of a country philosopher. [In Young, Arthur, *Rural Oeconomy*. See Morgan 4359]

Luther, Martin. The shorter Catechism of Dr. Martin Luther, translated from the Latin into English by a Clergyman of the Church of England; and now published together with the German . . . by G. A. Wachsel. London.

Toze, Eobald. The Present State of Europe; exhibiting a view of the natural and civil history of the several countries and kingdoms. Translated from the German by T. Nugent. 3 Vols. London.

United Brethren. Articles agreed upon by those members of the Unitas Fratrum whose names are hereunto subscribed, making provision for the support of their widows. Philadelphia. Printed by Henry Miller. [English and German]

Wolff, Christian Freiherr von. Logic, or Rational Thoughts on the powers of the human understanding; with their use and application in the knowledge and search of truth. Translated from the German of Baron Wolfius. To which is prexfixed a life of the Author. London.

BIBLIOGRAPHY OF WORKS
RELATING TO THIS STUDY

This bibliography contains material directly related to German influences in England, but does not contain general histories, editions of author's works, lexicons, or other general reference material. For example, it includes Peter Malekin's article, "Jacob Boehme's Influence on William Law," but does not contain Henri Talon's book, *William Law, a Study in Literary Craftsmanship*, although Talon's book does contain some material on the Boehme influence. It also does not contain works primarily concerned with English influences in Germany, such as the many works on this topic by Lawrence M. Price. Although some English Romantic poets are mentioned in the text, the bibliography does not contain material specifically concerned with the Romantic period. In addition to works I have consulted, the bibliography contains several works whose titles bear directly on Anglo-German studies to which I have not had access.

Abbey, Charles J. and Overton, John H. *The English Church in the Eighteenth Century.* (London, 1878).
Abbey, Charles John. *The English Church and its Bishops* 1700-1800. (London, 1887).
Alberti, G. W. *Briefe betreffend den allerneuesten Zustand der Religion und der Wissenschaften in Gross-Brittanien.* 4 Volumes. (Hanover, 1752-54).
Allen, Don Cameron. "Early eighteenth-century Literary Relations between England and Germany," *MLN* 49 (1934). 99-101.
Althaus, Friedrich. "Beiträge zur Geschichte der deutschen Colonie in England," *Unsere Zeit*, Neue Folge, 9. Jahrgang, Erste Hälfte, Leipzig, 1873.
Arnold, R. "Englische und deutsche Literatur," *Canadian Modern Language Review*, 13 (1957), 10-20.
Arundell, Dennis. *The Critic at the Opera.* (London, 1957).
Bailey, Margaret L. *Milton and Jakob Boehme, A Study of German Mysticism in* 17th *Century England.* (New York, 1914).
Barnett, Pamela R. *Theodore Haak, F. R. S.* (1605-1690); *the First German Translator of 'Paradise Lost'.* (The Haugue, 1962).
Batt, M. "Contributions to the History of English Opinion of German Literature. I. Gillies and the Foreign Quarterly Review. II. Gilies and Blackwood's Magazine," *MLN*, 17 (1902 and 18 (1903).
Beauchamp, William Martin. *Moravian Journals Relating to Central New York* 1745-66. (Syracuse, N.Y., 1916).
Benson, Louis F. *The English Hymn.* (London, 1916).
Benthem, Heinrich Ludolff. *Neu-eröffneter Engeländischer Kirch- und Schulen-Staat.* (Leipzig, 1932). [Lüneburg, 1694].
Bett, Henry. *The Hymns of Methodism.* (London, 1956).

Betts, E. "The Operatic Criticism of the Tattler and the Spectator," *Musical Quarterly*, 31 (1945), 318-330.

Beyer, Werner. "The Background of Coleridge's *Cain*, Precursor of 'The Ancient Mariner'," *Notes and Queries*, 3 (1956), 32-34, 82-84.

— "Coleridge's Early Knowledge of German," *Modern Philology*, 52 (1955), 192-200.

Bisset, Andrew. *Memoirs and Papers of Sir Andrew Mitchell*. (London, 1850). [This is a selection and is politically oriented. The complete papers in the British Museum have never been edited.]

Boehm, Anton Wilhelm. *Anton Wilhelm Böhmens, Weyland seiner Königlichen Hoheit, Prinz Georgens von Dännemarck, Hof-Predigers zu London, Sämtliche Erbauliche Schriften . . . ins Teutsche übersetzet worden . . . von Johann Jacob Rambach*. (Altona, 1731).

— *. . . Erbaulicher Schriften Andrer Theil . . . und mit einer Vorrede begleitet worden von einem Nieder-Sächsischen Theologo*. (Altona, 1733).

— *. . . Erbauliche Briefe, welche in teutscher, lateinischer und englischer Sprache von ihm geschrieben worden, mit einer Vorrede*. (Altona, 1737).

Brie, Friedrich. "Eulenspiegel in England," *Palaestra*, 27 (1903).

Burckhardt, J. G. *Kirchen-Geschichte der deutschen Gemeinden in London*. (Tübingen, 1798).

Burgess, W. P. *Wesleyan Hymnology*. (London, 1845).

Byrom, John. *A Catalogue of the Library of the Late John Byrom*. (London, 1848).

— *The Private Journal and Literary Remains of John Byrom*. Edited by Richard Parkinson. (London, 1854).

— *Selections from the Journals and Papers of John Byrom*. Edited by Henri Talon. (London, 1950).

A Catalogue of the Library at King's Cliffe Northamptonshire, founded by William Law, M.A. 1752. (King's Cliffe, 1927).

Charles, Robert Alan. *French Intermediaries in the Transmission of German Literature and Culture to England, 1750-1815*. (Diss. Penn. State, 1952).

Closs, Karl. "Jacob Boehmes Aufnahme in England," *Archiv für das Studium der neueren Sprachen und Literaturen*, 148 (1925).

Colwell, W. A. *German Literature in England 1750-1800*. (Diss. Harvard, 1906).

Creamer, D. *Methodist Hymnology*. (New York, 1848).

Davis, Edward Z. *Translations of German Poetry in American Magazines, 1741-1810*. (Philadelphia, 1905).

Duffield, Samuel Willoughby. *English Hymns: Their Authors and History*. (New York and London, 1886).

Ederheimer, Edgar. *Jakob Böhme und die Romantiker*. (Heidelberg, 1904).

Esch, Arno. *Englishe religiöse Lyrik des 17. Jahrhunderts*. (Tübingen, 1955).

Fairchild, Hoxie Neale. *Religious Trends in English Poetry*. 2 Volumes. (New York, 1939).

— "Romanticism and the Religious Revival in England," *JHI*, 2 (1941), 330-338.

Faust, Albert Bernhardt. *The German Element in the United States*. (Boston and New York, 1909).

Flaherty, M. Gloria. *In Defense of the Opera: a Survey of German Critical Writings on Opera from 1678 to 1770*. (Diss. Johns Hopkins Univ., 1965).

Fritz, Ernst. *Die Schweiz als geistige Mittlerin von Muralt bis Jacob Burckhardt*. (Zurich, 1932).

Füssli, Johann Heinrich. *Briefe*, hrsg. von Walter Muschg. (Basel, 1942).

Gagey, Edmond McAdoo. *Ballad Opera*. (New York, 1937).

Geissendoerfer, John T., ed. *Briefe an August Hermann Francke*. Illinois Studies in Language and Literature, 25 (1939).

Gem, Samuel Harvey. *The Mysticism of William Law*. (London, 1907).

Gill, Frederick C. *The Romantic Movement and Methodism*. (London, 1937).

Goodnight, Scott Holland, and Haertel, Martin Henry. *German Literature in American Magazines Prior to 1846*. (Madison, 1907).

Green, Vivian Hubert Howard. *The Young Mr. Wesley*. (London, 1961).

Gudde, Erwin Gustav. "Grimmelshausen's *Simplicius Simplicissimus* and Defoe's *Robinson Crusoe*," *Philological Quarterly*, 4 (1925), 110-120.

Haller, Albrecht von. *Tagebücher seiner Reisen nach Deutschland, Holland und England*, 1723-1727. (St. Gallen, 1948).

Haney, John Louis. "German Literature in England before 1790," *Americana Germanica*, 4 (1902), 130-154. [actually covers 1760-1790]

Harper, Kenneth, "Law and Wesley," *Church Quarterly Review*, 163 (1961), 61-71.

Harris, W. J. *The First Printed Translations into English of Great Foreign Classics*. (New York, 1909).

Harvey, F. B., "Methodism and the Romantic Movement," *London Quarterly*, July, 1934, 289-302.

Hatfield, James Taft, "John Wesley's Translations of German Hymns," *PMLA*, 11 (1896), 171-199.

Hedge, F. H., "Count Zinzendorf and the Moravians," *Martin Luther and Other Essays*, (Boston, 1888).

Hennig, John. "Simplicius Simplicissimus' British Relations," *MLR* 41 (1945), 34-45.

Herbert, Thomas Walter. *John Wesley as Editor and Author*. (Princeton, London, and Oxford, 1940).

Herford, Charles Harold. *Studies in the Literary Relations of England and Germany in the Sixteenth Century*. (Cambridge, 1886).

Herzfeld, Georg. "William Taylor von Norwich," *Studien zur Englischen Philologie*, 2 (1897).

— "Zur Geschichte der deutschen Literatur in England," *Archiv für das Studium der neueren Sprachen*, 105 (1900) 30 ff. and 110 (1903) 109 ff.

Hewitt, Theodore Brown. *Paul Gerhardt as a Hymn Writer and his Influence on English Hymnody*. (New Haven, 1918). [Taken from Julian's Dictionary of Hymnology.]

Hobhouse, Stephen, "Fides et Ratio," *Journal of Theological Studies*, 37 (1936), No. 148. [On William Law's first introduction to Jacob Boehme.]

— *William Law and eighteenth-century Quakerism*. (London, 1927).

Horn, David Bayne. *British Diplomatic Representatives* 1689-1789. (London, 1932).

Horneck, Philip. *The High German Doctor*. (London, 1714-1715). [A periodical consisting of two volumes of fifty numbers each. Reprinted 1715-1719].

Horning, E. *Evidences of Romantic Treatment of Religious Elements in Late 18th Century Minor Poetry* (1771-1800). (Catholic U. of Amer., 1932).

Hughes, Charles W. "John Christopher Pepusch," *Musical Quarterly*, 31 (1945), 54-70.

Huober, Hans-Günther, "Zinzendorfs Kirchenliederdichtung," *Germanische Studien*, 150 (1934).

Hutton, James E. *A History of the Moravian Church*. (London, 1909).

Jacobs, Henry Eyster. "The German Emigration to America 1709-1740," *The Pennsylvania-German Society Proceedings* and Adresses, 8 (1898).

— *A History of the Evangelical Lutheran Church in the United States*. (New York, 1893).

Jacoby, Karl. *Die ersten moralischen Wochenschriften Hamburgs am Anfange des 18. Jahrhunderts*. (Hamburg, 1888).

Jantz, Harold. "German Thought and Literature in New England, 1620-1820," *JEGP*, 41 (1942), 1-45.

— "German Baroque Literature," *MLN*, 57 (1962), 337-367.

— "Brockes' Poetic Apprenticeship," *MLN*, 57 (1962), 439-442.

Jones, Rufus M. *Spiritual Reformers in the 16th and 17th Centuries*. (Boston, 1914).

Julian, John. *A Dictionary of Hymnology*. (London, 1892).

Kelly, John Alexander. *England and the Englishmen in German Literature of the Eighteenth Century*. (New York, 1921).

— *German Visitors to English Theaters in the Eighteenth Century*. (Princeton, 1936).

Kenwood, Sydney H. "Lessing in England," *MLR* 9 (1914), 197-212 and 344-358.

Koch, E. E. *Geschichte des Kirchenlieds und Kirchengesangs der Christlichen, insbesondere der deutschen evangelischen Kirche*. (Stuttgart, 1852).

Koepp, W. *Johann Arndt*. (Berlin, 1912).

— *Untersuchung über die Mystik im Luthertum*. (Berlin, 1912).

Koeppel, E. "Deutsche Strömungen in der englischen Literatur," *English Monographs*, 122 (1910). [Nothing between Luther and Lessing]

136

L., C. F. "Deutsche Dichtungen in englischen Ubersetzungen," *Grenzboten*, 28. Jahrgang, II. Semester, II Band, (1869), 285.

Law, William. *Selected Mystical Writings of William Law, edited with Notes and twenty-four Studies in the Mystical Theology of William Law and Jacob Boehme and an Enquiry into the Influence of Jacob Boehme on Isaac Newton by Stephen Hobhouse.* Foreword by Aldous Huxley. 2nd Rev. Ed. (New York, 1948).

Lediard, Thomas. *The German Spy.* (London, 1738).

Levin, Harry. *The Broken Column: A Study in Romantic Hellenism.* (Cambridge, Mass., 1931).

Lightwood, James T. "Notes on the Foundery Tune-Book," *Wesley Historical Society Proceedings*, II.

Lodge, Sir Richard. *Great Britain and Prussia in the Eighteenth Century.* (Oxford, 1923).

Magnus, Laurie. *English Literature in its Foreign Relations 1300-1800.* (London and New York, 1927).

Malekin, Peter, "Jacob Boehme's Influence on William Law," *Studia Neophologia*, 36 (1964), 245-260.

Malin, William Gunn. *Catalogue of Books Relating to, or Illustrating the History of the Unitas Fratrum, or United Brethern.* (Philadelphia, 1881). [A very important catalogue which lists not only the German literature in English translation, but also the German literature published at the Moravian presses in England.]

Manikowsky, Fritz. *Die Welt- und Lebensanschauung in dem "Irdischen Vergnügen in Gott" von Barthold Heinrich Brockes.* (Greifswald Diss., 1914).

Marcus, H. *Friedrich der Grosse in der englischen Literatur.* (Leipzig, 1930).

Margraf, Ernst. *Einfluss der deutschen Literatur auf die englische am Ende des achtzehnten Jahrhunderts und im ersten Drittel des neunzehnten Jahrhunderts.* (Leipzig, 1901).

Mason, Eudo C. "Heinrich Füssli und Winckelmann," *Unterscheidung und Bewahrung*, 48 (1962), 232-258.

Milburn, Douglas, L., Jr. *German Drama in England: 1750-1850; with a List of German Plays Published and Performed.* (Diss., Rice, 1964).

Morgan, Bayard Q. *A Critical Bibliography of German Literature in English Translation 1481-1927 and Supplement 1928-1955.* (New York, 1965).

Morgan, Bayard Q. and Hohlfeld, Alexander R. *German Literature in British Magazines 1750-1860.* (Madison, 1949).

Muses, Charles Arthur. *Illumination on Jacob Boehme: The Works of Dionysius Andreas Freher.* (New York, 1951).

Nelle, Wilhelm. *Geschichte des deutschen evangelischen Kirchenliedes.* (Hamburg, 1909).

Nielsen, J. L. *John Wesley und das deutsche Kirchenlied.* (Bremen, 1938).

Odom, Herbert H. "The Estrangement of Celestial Mechanics and Religion," *Journal of the History of Ideas*, 27 (1966), 533-548.

Okely, Francis. *Memoirs of . . . Jacob Behmen.* (London, 1780). [Translated from several German writers.]

Osmond, Percy H. *The Mystical Poets of the English Church.* (London, 1919).

Oswald, E. "Der Einfluss des deutschen Schriftentums auf England," *Magazin für die Literatur des Auslandes*, Sept. 13, 1879.

Perry, Thomas Sergeant. "German Influence in English Literature," *Atlantic Monthly*, 40 (1877), 129.

Petersen, Christian. "Die Teutsch-übende Gesellschaft in Hamburg," *Zeitschrift des Hamburger Geschichtsvereins*, 2 (1847).

Pochmann, Henry A. and Schultz, Arthur R. *Bibliography of German Culture in America to 1940.* (Madison, 1954).

Pochmann, Henry A. *German Culture in America 1600-1900.* (Madison, 1957).

Popp, Karl Robert. *Boehme und Isaac Newton.* (Leipzig, 1935).

Purdie, Edna. "German Influence on the Literary Ballad in England during the Romantic Revial," *Publications of the English Goethe Society*, Series 2, 3 (1924), 97-119.

Reed, Bertha. *The Influence of Solomon Gessner upon English Literature.* (Philiadelphia, 1905).

Reed, Edward Bliss. *English Lyrical Poetry from its Origins to the Present Time.* (New Haven, London, and Oxford, 1912).

137

Reeves, Jeremiah Bascom. *The Hymn as Literature.* (New York and London, 1924).
Robson-Scott, William Douglas. *German Travellers in England* 1400-1800. (Oxford, 1953).
Roellinger, Francis X. "Intimations of Winckelmann in Paters Diaphaneité," *ELN*, 2 (1964), 277-282.
Rossel, Virgile. *Histoire des Relations Litteraires entre la France et L'Allemagne.* (Paris, 1897).
Schaible, Karl Heinrich. *Deutschen in England von den ersten germanischen Ansiedlungen in Britannien bis zum Ende des* 18. *Jahrhunderts.* (Strassburg, 1855).
Schirmer, Walter Franz. *Der Einfluss der deutschen Literatur auf die englische im* 19. *Jahrhundert.* (Halle, 1947).
Schmitt, Bernadotte Everly. *England and Germany* 1740-1914. (Princeton, 1918).
Schoeffler, H. *Protestantismus u. Literatur. Neue Wege z. englischen Literatur d.* 18. *Jh.* 1922.
— "Das Literarische Zürich (1700-1750)," *Die Schweiz im deutschen Geistesleben,* 40 (1925).
Scholes, Percy Alfred. *The Puritans and Music in England and New Ebgland.* (London, 1934).
Schulz, W. *Die Bedeutung der vom angelsächsischen Methodismus beeinflussten Liederdichtung für unsere deutschen Kirchengesänge.* (Greifswald Diss., 1934).
Schulze, Walter. "Die Quellen der Hamburg Oper (1678-1738)," *Hamburg Staats-und Universitäts-Bibliothek,* Neue Folge, Bd. 4.
Shepherd, Thomas Boswell. *Methodism and the Literature of the Eighteenth Century.* (London, 1940).
Sherwood, Margaret. *Undercurrents of Influence in English Romantic Poetry.* (Cambridge, Mass., 1934).
Shumway, Daniel B. "Egestorff's Translation of Klopstock's *Messias* Compared with other early English Translations," *Americana Germanica,* 3 (1899), 284-304.
Spurgeon, Caroline Frances Eleanor. *Mysticism in English Literature.* (Cambridge, 1913).
— "William Law and the Mystics," *Cambridge History of English Literature,* 9 (1912), Chap. 12.
Stephen, Leslie. "The Importation of German," *Studies of a Biographer,* 2 (1904), 38-76.
Stern, Bernard H. *The Rise of Romantic Hellenism in English Literature,* 1732-86. (Menasha, Wis., 1940).
Stockley, Violet A. *German Literature as Known in England* 1750-1830. (London, 1929).
Stokoe, F. W. *German Influence in the English Romantic Period.* (Cambridge, 1926).
Stimson, Dorothy. *Scientists and Amateurs. A History of the Royal Society.* (New York, 1948).
Strange, E. *Inquiry into the Rise and Establishment of the Royal Academy.* (London, 1795).
Struck, Wilhelm. *Der Einfluss Boehmes auf die englische Literatur des* 17. *Jahrhunderts.* (Berlin, 1936).
Süpfle, T. "Beiträge zur Geschichte der deutschen Literatur in England im letzten Drittel des 18. Jahrhunderts," *Zeitschrift für vergleichende Litteraturgeschichte,* Neue Folge, 6. Band, 1893, 305.
Thune, Nils. *The Behmenists and the Philadelphians.* (Uppsala, 1948).
Todt, Wilhelm. "Lessing in England," *Anglistische Arbeiten,* 1 (1912).
Tucker, Thomas George. *The Foreign Debt of English Literature.* (London, 1907).
Umbach, Emil. *Die deutschen Moralischen Wochenschriften und der Spectator von Addison und Steele, ihre Beziehungen zu einander und zur deutschen Literatur des* 18. *Jahrhunderts.* (Diss., Strassburg, 1911).
Vetter, Theodor. *Zürich als Vermittlerin englischer Literatur im achtzehnten Jahrhundert.* (Zürich, 1891).
Walz, John A. *German Influence in American Education and Culture.* (Philadelphia, 1936).
Wasserman, Earl R. "Nature Moralized: The Divine Analogy in the Eighteenth Century," *ELH* 20 (1953), 39 ff.
Wauer, Gerhard Adolf. *Die Anfänge der Brüderkirche in England.* (Leipzig, 1900).
Webb, Daniel. *Untersuchungen des Schönen in der Mahlerey.* Aus dem Englischen Uberstzt. (Zürich, 1766). [*Vorrede* by Füssli important]
Weddingen, Otto. "Die Vermittler deutschen Geistes in England und Nordamerika," *Archiv für das Studium der neueren Sprachen und Literaturen,* 59 (1878), 129-154.

138

Wesley, Charles. *The Journal of the Reverend Charles Wesley.* (London, 1910).
Wesley, John. *The Journal of the Reverend John Wesley.* (London and New York, 1907).
— *The Letters of the Reverend John Wesley.* Ed. by John Telford. (London, 1931).
Whitley, William. *Congregational Hymn Singing.* (London, 1933).
Wieden, Fritz. *Samuel Taylor Coleridge as a Student of German Literature.* (Diss., Toronto, 1963).
Wilkens, Frederick H. "Early Influence of German Literature in America," *Americana Germanica*, 3 (1899), 103-205.
— "G.H.C. Egestorff's First Stay in England and his Translation of Klopstock's Messiah," *Americana Germanica*, 4 (1902), 192 ff.
Wormhoudt, Arthur. *Jacob Boehme's Influence on William Law.* (Diss., Univ. of Iowa, 1943).
— "Newton's Natural Philosophy in the Behmenistic Works of William Law," *Journal of the History of Ideas*, 10 (1949), 411-429.
Zeiger, Theodor. *Beiträge zur Geschichte des Einflusses der neueren deutschen Litteratur auf die englische.* (Berlin, 1901).
Zeydel, Edwin H. "The Teaching of German in the United States from Colonial Times to the Present," *German Quarterly*, 37 (1964), 315-391.

INDEX

REPRINTS FROM OUR COMPARATIVE LITERATURE STUDIES

Through the University of North Carolina Press
Chapel Hill, North Carolina 27514

2. Werner P. Friederich. DANTE'S FAME ABROAD, 1350-1850. The Influence of Dante Alighieri on the Poets and Scholars of Spain, France, England, Germany, Switzerland and the United States. Rome, 1950; Third Printing 1966. Pp. 584. Paper, $ 10.00.
10. Charles E. Passage. DOSTOEVSKI THE ADAPTER. A Study in Dostoevski's Use of the Tales of Hoffmann. 1954. Reprinted 1963. Pp. x, 205. Paper, $ 3.50. Cloth, $ 4.50.
11. Werner P. Friederich and David H. Malone. OUTLINE OF COMPARATIVE LITERATURE. From Dante Alighieri to Eugene O'Neill. 1954. Fourth Printing, 1967. Pp. 460. Paper, $ 6.50.

Through Russell and Russell, Inc.
Publishers, 122 East 42nd Street
New York, New York 10017

1. Fernand Baldensperger and Werner P. Friederich. BIBLIOGRAPHY OF COMPARATIVE LITERATURE. 1950. Pp. 729. Cloth, $ 15.00.
6. 7, 9, 14, 16, 18, 21, 25 and 27. W. P. Friederich and H. Frenz (eds): YEARBOOKS OF COMPARATIVE AND GENERAL LITERATURE. Vols. I (1952) to IX (1960). Cloth, $ 7.50 per volume.

Through Johnson Reprint Corporation
111 Fifth Avenue
New York, New York 10003

3. R. C. Simonini, Jr. ITALIAN SCHOLARSHIP IN RENAISSANCE ENGLAND. Cloth, $ 12.50.
4. GOETHE'S SORROWS OF YOUNG WERTER, TRANSLATED BY GEORGE TICKNOR. Edited with Introduction and Critical Analysis by Frank G. Ryder. Cloth, $ 8.00.
5. Helmut A. Hatzfeld. A CRITICAL BIBLIOGRAPHY OF THE NEW STYLISTICS APPLIED TO THE ROMANCE LITERATURES, 1900-1952. Cloth, $ 12.00.
15. Dorothy B. Schlegel. SHAFTESBURY AND THE FRENCH DEISTS. Cloth, $ 12.50.
19. P. A. Shelley, A. O. Lewis Jr. and W. W. Betts Jr., eds. ANGLO-GERMAN AND AMERICAN-GERMAN CROSSCURRENTS, Volume One. Cloth, $ 15.00.
22. Harvey W. Hewett-Thayer. AMERICAN LITERATURE AS VIEWED IN GERMANY, 1818-1861. Cloth $ 8.50.
23-24. Werner P. Friederich, ed. COMPARATIVE LITERATURE: PROCEEDINGS OF THE SECOND CONGRESS OF THE INTERNATIONAL COMPARATIVE LITERATURE ASSOCIATION, 2 vols. Cloth $ 45.00.
26. DANTE'S LA VITA NUOVA, TRANSLATED BY RALPH WALDO EMERSON. Edited and annotated by J. Chesley Mathews. Cloth, $ 8.00.
28. Haskell M. Block, ed. THE TEACHING OF WORLD LITERATURE. Cloth, $ 6.00.
30. Oskar Seidlin. ESSAYS IN GERMAN AND COMPARATIVE LITERATURE. Cloth, $ 10.00.
34. William A. McQueen and Kiffin A. Rockwell. THE LATIN POETRY OF ANDREW MARVELL. Introduction, Original Text and Translation. Cloth, $ 8.50.